Peabody Journal of Education

T0347094

Camilla Benbow, Dean, Peabody College
James Guthrie, Editor
Michele Thompson, Coordinating Editor
Matthew Springer, Associate Editor

Peabody
Journal
of Education

Volume 79, Number 4, 2004

Assessing Teacher, Classroom, and School Effects

(continued)

Book Notes

PEABODY JOURNAL OF EDUCATION, 79(4), 1–3
ISBN 978-0-8058-9524-7

Introduction to the Special Issue: Assessing Teacher, Classroom, and School Effects

Allan Odden
Consortium for Policy Research in Education
University of Wisconsin—Madison

The six articles in this guest-edited issue of the *Peabody Journal of Education* focus generally on new directions in assessing and measuring teacher, classroom, and school effects on improvements in student academic achievement and more specifically analyze the criterion validity and surrounding human resources strategies of new efforts to implement performance-based teacher evaluations, the results of which in some cases are linked to new knowledge- and skills-based teacher salary schedules.

The first article, by Odden, Borman, and Fermanich, provides a general conceptual framework for the three articles that follow it. Odden et al.

The research reported in this article was supported by a grant from the U.S. Department of Education, Office of Educational Research and Improvement, National Institute on Educational Governance, Finance, Policymaking, and Management to the Consortium for Policy Research in Education (CPRE) and the Wisconsin Center for Education Research, School of Education, University of Wisconsin–Madison (Grant OERI–R308A60003). The opinions expressed are those of the authors and do not necessarily reflect the view of the National Institute on Educational Governance, Finance, Policymaking, and Management, Office of Educational Research and Improvement, U.S. Department of Education; the institutional partners of CPRE; or the Wisconsin Center for Education Research.

Requests for reprints should be sent to Allan Odden, University of Wisconsin–Madison, Consortium for Policy Research in Education, 1025 West Johnson Street, Madison, WI 53706. E-mail: arodden@wisc.edu argue that assessing the individual effects of teacher, classroom, and school factors on improvements in student learning requires two major shifts in research. The first is to measure key teacher/classroom and school factors that theory and other research show should be linked to student learning; the second shift is to analyze them collectively in a multilevel framework using some type of hierarchical linear modeling technique. Odden et al.'s article shows that the bulk of research to date assesses individually the impacts of certain, usually single teacher, classroom and school variables on student learning and usually in isolation from all the other variables. In the article, Odden et al. argue that there are certain factors in education that should significantly impact student learning—the curriculum that is taught, how that curriculum is taught, the quality of the individual doing the teaching, and the instructional environment of the school and classrooms within which that instruction takes place; the goal is to create over time an "educational model" of educational effects.

The next three articles use this general framework to study the criterion validity of new performance-based teacher evaluation systems, which provides one measure of teacher quality. The Milanowski article studies the system in Cincinnati, Ohio, the results of which were initially to be linked to a performance pay structure; the Kimball, White, Milanowski, and Borman article studies the system in Washoe County (Reno, Nevada) that is not linked to pay; and the Gallagher article analyzes the system in the Vaughn Charter School in Los Angeles. All three places use some version of the teaching standards and evaluation rubrics developed by Charlotte Danielson (1996), which produce four levels of teacher practice. All three articles show that the evaluation systems have significant elements of criterion validity—that is, the higher the evaluation scores, the greater the student learning gains made in those teachers' classrooms. Although the magnitude of the results vary by district, school, subject area, and grade level, and more research needs to be conducted, the findings show that valid performance-based evaluation systems can be designed and implemented and provide one measure of teacher quality that is linked to student learning gains.

Heneman and Milanowski argue in their article, however, that the human resources (HR) systems within which these ambitious evaluation and compensation systems are managed need to be strengthened. The Heneman and Milanowski article develops a model of what a strategic and comprehensive HR system would include in education and unfortunately shows that neither of the jurisdictions that operated these new evaluation and compensation initiatives really embedded them within a supportive and comprehensive HR system, although the strengths of the HR systems varied across each of the three jurisdictions. Heneman and

Milanowski's article includes suggestions for how better HR systems could be developed.

The last article by Odden outlines a set of "lessons learned" from these five articles, focusing largely on the lessons learned about designing, implementing, and using performance-based evaluation systems that could be linked to teacher pay increases. Although admitting that much more research is needed on these systems, Odden concludes that the systems are "good enough" to use for significant consequences, such as a pay increase or a promotion, and encourages other schools, districts, and states to engage in similar efforts—all designed to improve instructional practice in ways that produce greater improvements in student academic achievement.

Reference

Danielson, C. (1996). *Enhancing professional practice: A framework for teaching.* Alexandria, VA: Association for Supervision and Curriculum Development.

PEABODY JOURNAL OF EDUCATION, 79(4), 4–32

Assessing Teacher, Classroom, and School Effects, Including Fiscal Effects

Allan Odden and Geoffrey Borman

Educational Leadership and Policy Analysis
University of Wisconsin–Madison

Mark Fermanich

Educational Leadership and Special Education
Sonoma State University

In this article, we argue that too much previous research has tended to assess the effects of student, classroom, and school variables in isolation from other variables and has often used statistical techniques that ignored the nested nature of the 3 classes of factors. We then argue that a more educationally oriented framework should be used to assess the effects of various student, classroom/teacher, and school variables on student learning, particularly student learning gains, and we identify several variables within each class of

The research reported in this article was supported by a grant from the U.S. Department of Education, Office of Educational Research and Improvement, National Institute on Educational Governance, Finance, Policymaking, and Management to the Consortium for Policy Research in Education (CPRE) and the Wisconsin Center for Education Research, School of Education, University of Wisconsin–Madison (Grant OERI–R308A60003). The opinions expressed are those of the authors and do not necessarily reflect the view of the National Institute on Educational Governance, Finance, Policymaking, and Management, Office of Educational Research and Improvement, U.S. Department of Education; the institutional partners of CPRE; or the Wisconsin Center for Education Research.

Requests for reprints should be sent to Allan Odden, University of Wisconsin–Madison, Consortium for Policy Research in Education, 1025 West Johnson Street, Madison, WI 53706. E-mail: arodden@wisc.edu

4

factors that research so far has identified. In the article, we suggest some standard hierarchical linear modeling models that could be used to conduct analyses that do account for the nested nature of all variables.

In a then unique chapter in an annual yearbook of the American Education Finance Association (AEFA), Cohen wrote in 1983 about instructional, management, and organizational conditions in effective schools. The yearbook was an initial effort by AEFA to link the program side of education with the finance side, an effort that took center stage in the late 1990s as "adequacy" began to dominate the school finance policy landscape (Minorini & Sugarman, 1999). Cohen, who had been a program officer overseeing effective schools research in the old National Institute of Education and became Assistant Secretary for Elementary and Secondary Education in the late 1990s, sought to synthesize the literatures of what then was termed *effective teaching* and *effective schools* research. Cohen's chapter was one of the first to set the findings of those different but related research efforts into a "nested" framework that included both teacher/classroom and school effects. With hindsight, educators can now see that Cohen was suggesting that they should think about and study school, teacher, and student effects in a multilevel framework which recognizes that improvements in student learning emerge from three different arenas and, in statistical terms, levels of the education system—the student, the classroom, and the school.

Since the 1980s, moreover, researchers have recognized that statistical models must be designed to represent and measure this complex multilevel structure of schools (Bryk & Raudenbush, 1988; Burstein, 1980; Raudenbush & Bryk, 1986). In these studies, the researchers argued that estimating the magnitudes of such effects should be accomplished using hierarchical linear models (HLMs), which formally represent students, classrooms, and schools as distinct units or levels of analysis. Unfortunately, insufficient research has been conducted either using this general three-level framework, which nests students within classrooms and classrooms within schools, or specifically using an HLM approach to capture fully this three-level structure.

Further, too much research has attempted to focus on single variables in analyzing what impacts student learning gains. Some studies, within a psychological or sociological framework, have focused on student variables, such as motivation, persistence, or social stratification by race or social class, and ignored classroom and school variables altogether. Other studies, even the effective teaching studies, have focused on classroom or instructional factors and virtually ignored student and school effects (e.g., Ehrenberg & Brewer 1994, 1995; Monk & King, 1994; Wayne & Youngs, 2003). Still other studies have addressed school factors but ignored classroom and student variables (e.g., Sorenson & Hallinan, 1977). Finally, economic production function studies might include a range of student, classroom, school, and even district factors but rarely have they been analyzed in a multilevel model, and too often they have used district averages for these factors (e.g., Monk, 1994; Rice, 2001).

These research shortcomings need to be rectified. Cohen, Burstein, Bryk, and Raudenbush were correct in their 1980s articles that school and classroom effects should be studied in a multilevel schema. Moreover, we argue in this article that we need a more general educational model with a series of educationally oriented variables that include key school, classroom, and student factors to more accurately estimate various school and classroom impacts on improvements in student learning over time. We need such a model both substantively to determine more accurate estimates of the effects of such factors at different levels in the education system and financially to progress toward ensuring that fiscal investments support practices that have an evidence base. Long term, using multilevel statistical techniques in a fully developed educational model should help give more substance to research that attempts to determine the cost of "educational adequacy." Further, with the federal No Child Left Behind Act of 2001 that requires states to test all students each year in Grades 3 through 8, we should be able to conduct appropriate analyses of the impacts on student learning of numerous programs and strategies in elementary and secondary schools if we can collect the appropriate student, teacher/classroom, and school variables.

This article is divided into five sections. In the first three sections, we review the literature on teacher/classroom, school, and student effects to isolate the key school, classroom, and student factors that research has shown, usually independent of each other, to impact student learning. In the next section, we quickly summarize other research, such as economic production function research, that adds to our knowledge of school and classroom effects. Then, we propose a full educational model comprised of schools, classrooms, and students that should drive research in the next several years to sort out which of these variables have what magnitude of impacts on student learning. Finally, we show how the findings can be used to inform educational adequacy and the distribution and use of resources at the district and school levels.

Teacher and Classroom Effects

Recent research has shown that teacher and classroom effects on student learning are the largest in the education system (Goldhaber,

2002). In part, these findings have helped bolster the strong policy interest in teacher quality. Summarizing from several of his studies, Sanders (2000), who pioneered the Tennessee Value-Added Assessment System, stated that "differences in teacher effectiveness is the single largest factor affecting academic growth of populations of students" (p. 8). In other words, Sanders argued that teacher effects are larger than class size effects, spending differences, and several other factors believed to impact student learning. Contrasting teacher to school effects, Webster, Mendro, Orsak, and Weerasinghe (1996), in a similar value-added study of school and teacher effects in the Dallas Public Schools, concluded that a school's effect could actually represent an aggregation of the individual effects of its teachers. These claims are in part supported by other recent studies that have found differences in student achievement among classrooms within schools to be greater than the differences among schools (Hanushek, Kain, & Rivkin, 1998; Meyer, 2001; Webster et al., 1996). In a study of the Denver Public Schools, for example, again using multilevel statistical techniques, Meyer (2001) found that teachers accounted for more than twice the total variation in student test score changes than did schools.

These and related studies (Rivkin, Hanushek, & Kain, 2001; Rowan, Correnti, & Miller, 2002; Sanders & Horn, 1994; Sanders & Rivers, 1996; Wright, Horn, & Sanders, 1997) have largely documented variation in student learning gains among teacher and classrooms per se. Put differently, they have shown that (a) students learn differential amounts during a normal academic year depending on their teacher and (b) individual teachers consistently produce—year after year—low, medium, or high learning gains for their classrooms of students. In analyzing data from one large national survey, Rowan, Correnti, and Miller (2002) found that the differences in impact for the most effective teachers can be 9 months or more, essentially a full year of learning. Both Sanders (2000) and Webster, Mendro, Orsak, and Weerasinghe (1996, 1998) found similar effects for the top teachers (about one sixth of the total) and found that the bottom group of teachers (again about one sixth of the total) actually produces negative impacts on students; students with the bottom group of teachers decline over the year in their relative achievement. Indeed, Sanders argued that a student who is taught by an ineffective teacher for 2 years in a row can never recover the learning lost during those years.

In sum, quite a bit of recent research has shown that teachers have substantial impacts on student learning and that there is a large variation in the impact of individual teachers both across grade levels and within grade levels teaching the same subjects. The bottom line is that teacher and classroom effects are strong and large.

However, although these studies have documented that teachers and classrooms have variable impacts on student learning gains, most have not indicated what factors related to teachers/classrooms actually cause those impacts. What we really need to know is if there are particular characteristics of teachers that are associated with high and low impact as well as if there are particular things teachers do instructionally that produce higher or lower impacts on students. After recognizing that teachers matter greatly, the general hypothesis is that it is what teachers know and actually do in the classroom that affects what students learn.

Teacher Characteristics

Several research streams provide some beginning answers to this hypothesis. Most studies have shown that teachers' degrees and education units beyond a bachelor's degree rarely have an impact on student learning (Goldhaber & Brewer, 1997; Hanushek, 1986, 1989, 1992; Murnane, 1983). This same research has shown, moreover, that years of experience generally also have little impact but that teachers with 3 or more years of experience are more effective than less experienced teachers (Murnane, 1983). The literature on whether teacher licensure has an impact has been quite mixed (Darling-Hammond & Youngs, 2002; Goldhaber & Brewer, 1999, 2000). Research on whether a college major or the number of units taken in an academic area has an effect so far has suggested that such behavior in mathematics and to a lesser degree science impacts student achievement in those areas (Monk, 1994; Monk & King, 1994). In a review of the literature on teacher characteristics that are linked to student learning gains, Wayne and Youngs (2003) found that the following teacher characteristics had positive impacts on student learning:

- General measures of ability or academic talent such as an ACT, SAT, or licensure exam score (e.g., Ferguson, 1991, 1998; Ferguson & Ladd, 1996).
- Verbal ability (e.g., Ehernberg & Brewer, 1995; Hanushek, 1992).
- Coursework, certification, or a degree (either bachelor's or master's) in mathematics (and, to a lesser degree, science) for secondary teachers of those subjects (e.g., Goldhaber & Brewer, 1997; Monk & King, 1994; Rowan, Chiang, & Miller, 1997).
- Graduation from a higher quality college or university (Ehrenberg & Brewer, 1994; Goldhaber & Brewer, 1997; Summers & Wolfe, 1975, 1977).

These positive findings would suggest that future research on teacher effects should include these and other possible variables because it does seem that they can have separate and independent impacts. Teacher licensure should continue to be a variable studied, even though research has been mixed on the impact of this variable.

Teacher Classroom Practices

An educator would think that what teachers taught and how they taught it would impact student learning, and there is considerable support for this general hypothesis. Indeed, the research on tracking has generally argued that the major reason students in the "low" track learn less is that the curriculum that they are taught covers less content and requires less of the students cognitively (Gamoran, 1992, 1993, 1996, 1997, 1998).

Porter's research (Gamoran, Porter, Smithson, & White, 1997; Porter, 2002; Porter & Smithson, 2001) has addressed the issue of content taught in one of the most detailed ways. Porter and his colleagues developed survey instruments that measure what content teachers actually cover in their classrooms and the cognitive demand of that content. They found that topic coverage alone does not differentiate strongly among classrooms but that content coverage together with cognitive demand does. Porter (2002) found that teachers providing instruction better aligned to the test (topic by cognitive demand) produce more learning gains than do other teachers. Porter found correlations between this variable and gains in student achievement of between 0.4 and 0.5.

In terms of pedagogy, or instructional practice, the effective teaching research of the 1970s and 1980s (Brophy & Good, 1986; Rosenshine & Stevens, 1986) identified a series of teaching practices that were linked to student learning gains. Although this product–process research has been somewhat criticized during the past 10 years, the research had shown that certain teaching practices—for example, anticipatory set, direct instruction, wait time, time on task, homework for which students had a high rate of success, and so forth—did produce learning gains at least in the basic skills for students in schools with high concentrations of low-income and minority enrollment (Rosenshine & Stevens, 1986; Rowan, Chiang, & Miller, 1996).

Although Porter (1994, 1998, 2002) and others have had less success in measuring and linking pedagogical practices to learning gains using larger and more representative samples and more sophisticated statistical techniques, recent studies of a teacher's general pedagogical approach and behaviors have produced intriguing findings. For example, minority students may realize larger academic benefits from reductions in class size than their nonminority peers (Finn & Achilles, 1999; Krueger & Whitmore, 2001). Based on a larger review of teaching behaviors and student outcomes, Ferguson (1998) also suggested that teachers' beliefs, expectations, and behaviors may affect African American students more than Whites. Other research has found that "authentic pedagogy" or a focus on problem solving can produce increases in both basic skills as well as understanding and problem solving (Bransford, Brown, & Cocking, 1999; Bruer, 1993; Fennema & Romberg, 1999; Smith, Lee, & Newmann, 2001).

Moreover, as National Board for Professional Teaching Standards certification increases in use across the country, another variable could be whether a teacher is National Board certified. The argument by the Board is that such teachers should be more effective in teaching students, and studies are underway by Dan Goldhaber at the University of Washington to test this hypothesis.

Further, research on performance-based teacher evaluation systems has made connections between instruction and learning gains. A comprehensive, well-constructed teacher evaluation measure may potentially combine a number of elements affecting teacher effectiveness including content knowledge, teaching practices, classroom management skills, motivation, and the classroom context (Rowan et al., 1997). In part to test this conjecture, Gallagher (2004/this issue); Holtzapple (2001, 2002); Kimball, White, Milanowski, and Borman (2004/this issue); and Milanowski (2004/this issue) have studied places that have implemented such comprehensive evaluation systems—all adaptations of a teacher evaluation based on the Danielson (1996) Framework for Teaching. All of these studies documented via HLM techniques that teachers with higher evaluation scores produced larger learning gains in student achievement as measured by standardized tests. For example, using HLM, Gallagher found that teachers' average evaluation scores in literacy are a highly statistically significant predictor of student performance. For every point increase in teacher evaluation scores, student performance increases almost 13 points.

Finally, it should also be the goal to study more specific instructional practices. For example, Rowan's (1999) study of the effects of both general and subject-specific teaching practices found that four measures of general instructional practice had differing effects depending on the skills assessed by the test. The four measures were (a) emphasis on higher order thinking skills, (b) time spent presenting/explaining material, (c) time spent giving students feedback on performance, and (d) time spent leading discussion groups. The analysis showed that when the focus of the assessment was computational skills, a focus on higher order thinking skills had a negative effect of –0.05; time spent presenting/explaining material and time spent giving feedback had small positive effects of 0.045 and 0.06, respectively; and time spent leading discussion groups had no statistically significant effect. When the emphasis of the assessment was on math concepts and applications, time spent leading discussion groups had a small positive effect of 0.064, whereas the remaining three measures had no statistically significant effects (Rowan, 1999).

In the same study, Rowan (1999) also examined the effects of two reading-specific measures of practice: use of a phonetics-based text and a "reading for meaning" approach to teaching comprehension. These measures also resulted in small, although positive, effects. Use of a phonetics-based text had a positive effect of 0.025 *SD* in test scores and reading for meaning had a positive effect of 0.022 *SD*.

Taking a different approach, Heistad (1999) conducted a value-added teacher effects study of second grade reading in Minneapolis elementary schools and correlated the results with detailed survey data on teachers' reading-specific instructional practices. Heistad found distinct differences in the instructional approaches used by teachers who had significantly larger value-added effects on their students' reading achievement. These "exceptional" teachers, defined as teachers whose effect size ranked in the top 20% in at least 2 of the 3 years studied, were more likely to use phonics-based instruction, provide guided practice in the early stages of instruction, and emphasize the development of word attack strategies.

Further, in a study of teachers' practices from the Prospects data set, a national database on thousands of teachers in Grades 1, 3, and 7, Rowan, Correnti, and Miller (2002) reported the following positive and statistically significant effects of curriculum coverage variables on students' growth in reading: $d = 0.10$ for the effect of teacher's emphasis on word analysis skills, $d = 0.17$ for the effect of the reading comprehension measure, and $d = 0.18$ for the effect of a teacher's emphasis on the writing process. These effects were found using HLM growth models for the early grades cohort of the Prospects study. The effect of content coverage on early elementary student's growth in mathematics achievement was not statistically significant. However, there was a statistically significant relation for this variable for students in the upper elementary grades, with an effect size of $d = 0.09$ (both using a single, multi-item scale measuring content coverage).

Context

Additional studies have shown that the school or classroom context can also impact educational outcomes, other factors held constant. Schools and classrooms with higher concentrations of poor and minority students may introduce additional risks for students that go beyond their individual poverty or minority status and family background (Jencks & Mayer, 1990). Further, grouping practices within classrooms have separate and independent impacts. In some cases, multiage classrooms with homogeneous groupings across grade levels has more impact, as in reading achievement for Grades 1 through 3 (Slavin, 1987), and sometimes within-class grouping is a better strategy, as for elementary mathematics (Slavin, 1987; Slavin & Karweit, 1985). Moreover, sometimes neither grouping practices nor length of classrooms have positive or negative impacts on learning, such as "looping" in elementary schools (Pavan, 1992; Slavin, 1992; Veenman, 1995) or block schedules in high schools (Canady & Rettig, 1996). Studying the effects of all these context factors in a more comprehensively specified model of classroom and school effects is important.

Summary

From this quick review, we conclude that research shows generally that

1. Individual teachers have widely varying impacts on student learning gains so that including the classroom as a level in the education system is important as is gathering measures of what teachers know and do in their classroom.

2. Some teacher characteristics—for example, graduation from a high-quality college or university, verbal ability, scores on standardized tests including licensure tests, a major in mathematics and perhaps science for secondary teachers of those subjects, more than 3 years of experience, perhaps licensure in the subject taught—differentially impact student learning gains. Therefore, a model of educational effects should include a limited list of key teacher characteristics.

3. What teachers do in the classroom also matters. Content coverage together with the cognitive demand of that coverage is important as potentially are various measures of pedagogical practice. Therefore, measuring content covered, the cognitive demand of that content, and a variety of pedagogical practices used is important. Broader measures of instructional practice, such as direct or authentic instruction, National Board Certification, and a score on a comprehensive teacher evaluation should also be analyzed as should more specific, concrete practices used at specific grade levels to teach specific content areas.

Moreover, recent efforts to measure content covered at more microlevels (see Rowan, Camburn, & Richard, 2002; Rowan, Correnti, and Miller, 2002) using logs recording practice rather than end-of-year surveys appears to have shown that these variables, when more precisely measured, have even larger effects than those found in the work of Porter (2002).

4. Assessing context variables also is important. Classroom context includes socioeconomic characteristics of the classroom, specifically poverty and race variables, and student grouping practices.

We are aware that many of the studies of teacher and classroom effects have not included the school in their analyses, which may have caused the impact of teacher and classroom variables to be overstated or understated. However, the preceding teacher and classroom variables seem to be those that research over the past 20 years or so has generally found to impact student learning and should generally be the types of teacher and classroom variables included in research using a more comprehensive, three-level, and explicitly educational model of school, classroom, and student effects.

School Effects

There is a long tradition of research on school effects. Although most school effects research has focused just on the school and not on school effects together with classroom effects, the research nevertheless has identified several school-level factors that should be considered in developing a comprehensive model of school-, classroom-, and student-level effects on student learning.

The effective schools studies, referenced previously in the Cohen (1983) synthesis, typically have involved in-depth case studies of a small sample of schools in an effort to identify specific traits or processes shared by more effective schools (Purkey & Smith, 1983; Scheerens, Nanninga, & Pelgrum, 1989). In these process–product studies, the characteristics of high-scoring schools were compared to those of less effective schools, both usually in communities with high concentrations of low-income and minority students, and the commonalities among the effective schools were noted (Purkey & Smith, 1983). Well-known studies by Edmonds (1979); Brookover, Brady, and Flood (1979); and others have led to the development of a "five-factor" model of effective schools. This model identified five correlates that studies found consistently associated with effective schools (Scheerens et al., 1989):

1. Strong educational leadership, usually but not always by the principal.
2. An emphasis on teaching basic skills.
3. A safe and orderly school climate.
4. High expectations for students' achievement.
5. Frequent evaluation of students' progress.

Although the five-factor model has been elaborated over the years, it still forms the basis for much of the theory and thinking about school effectiveness research today (Scheerens et al., 1989). However, more recent research has begun to turn these factors into more generalized school variables. Rowan et al. (1996) identified several school situations (i.e., contextual variables such as class size, student grouping strategies, school climate, instructional leadership, and professional culture) in addition to teachers' knowledge, instructional practice, and motivation as key to educational effectiveness. Whereas the latter two categories of variables deal specifically with teachers as individuals and would be considered classroom variables, the contextual category refers to a school's capacity to support teachers in providing effective instruction.

The elements that compose Rowan et al.'s (1996) category of school and classroom contextual factors largely overlap with the effective schools correlates formulated by Edmonds (1979) and others (Purkey & Smith, 1983). Four of these elements of school capacity are particularly important. Two elements relate to school processes—school leadership and professional community. The other two elements, professional development and class size, relate to school resource use. Although class size is not generally cited in process–product research, its positive effect on student achievement in kindergarten through Grade 3 has been well documented in a number of studies (Finn, 2002; Grissmer, 1999, 2001; Hedges & Greenwald, 1996). Next we provide a brief discussion of the relevance of each of these elements to school capacity to support effective instruction.

School Leadership

The nature of the effect of principals' instructional leadership on school effectiveness has been long debated in terms of both effect size and form (Hallinger & Heck, 1996). However, most researchers and policymakers agree that principals play an important role in school success (Hallinger & Heck, 1996). This is particularly true for restructured schools in which Murphy (1994) identified a key role of the principal to be "enabling and supporting teacher success" (p. 31).

Although studies have found that principal leadership may account for between 2% and 8% of total variation in test scores among schools, research generally supports the notion that principals have little or no direct effect on student achievement but instead influence school success through indirect or mediated means (Hallinger & Heck, 1996). In particular, it is the principal's influence on a school's instructional climate and organization that is crucial. Principals influence the learning climate within which a school's teachers work by establishing clear instructional goals, providing programmatic coherence, communicating relevant information to their teaching staff, establishing accountability for student learning, fostering collaboration, and maintaining student discipline (Bossert, Dwyer,

Rowan, & Lee, 1982; Hallinger & Heck, 1998). They also support the professional growth of individual teachers through direct classroom supervision, including teacher observation and feedback, and professional development opportunities (Hallinger & Heck, 1998; Heck, Larsen, & Marcoulides, 1990).

Professional Community

Professional community, an aspect of a school's organizational culture, has been shown to increase the intellectual quality of instruction as well as overall student achievement by enhancing the organizational capacity of schools (Louis & Marks, 1998; Newmann & Wehlage, 1995). Newmann and Wehlage described professional community as possessing three general traits in which teachers (a) pursue a shared sense of purpose for student learning, (b) engage in collaborative activities to achieve this purpose, and (c) take collective responsibility for student learning. Others have identified deprivatization of practice and reflective dialogue as additional elements of professional community (Louis & Marks, 1998).

Shared sense of purpose refers to a consensus among school staff as to the mission of and principles by which the school operates. *Collaborative activity* describes the extent to which teachers engage in cooperative practices to achieve the school's goals. *Collective responsibility* refers to the degree to which all teachers share responsibility for the academic success of all of a school's students. *Deprivatization of practice* refers to the practice of teachers interacting professionally, for example, observing and providing feedback on each other's teaching. *Reflective dialogue* is the professional conversation teachers have about specific issues of instructional practice (Louis & Marks, 1998). Furthermore, the presence of professional community in a school is strongly influenced by certain organizational traits such as the quality of leadership, school size, teacher quality, school organization, and the degree to which schools have the authority to make operational decisions (Newmann & Wehlage, 1995).

Professional Development

There is growing recognition that effective professional development is essential for schools to meet the goals inherent in standards-based reform. As teachers face increasing expectations for results along with significantly changing school contexts, their schools must provide sufficient training and support to enable them to be successful. Studies of professional development spending in districts and schools have shown that a considerable amount is currently being invested in professional development but often not as part of an effective, coordinated strategy (Fermanich, 2002; Miles,

Odden, Fermanich, Archibald, & Gallagher, in press). Recent research has also made significant headway in identifying the essential elements of effective professional development (Corcoran, 1995; Desimone, Porter, Birman, Garet, & Yoon, 2002; Desimone, Porter, Garet, Yoon, & Birman, 2002; Elmore, 2002; Garet, Birman, Porter, Yoon, & Desimone, 2002; Little, 1993; Odden, Archibald, Fermanich, & Gallagher, 2002; Smylie, 1996; Sparks & Hirsh, 1999; Stigler & Hiebert, 1999):

- School based and job embedded.
- Sustained and ongoing.
- Collective participation of groups of teachers from the same school, department, or grade level.
- Focus on specific content and content-specific pedagogy.
- Opportunities for teachers to engage in active learning.
- Comprise a coherent approach to professional development that is aligned with a school's needs, standards, and goals.

Unfortunately, there is little research to date that specifically links investments in professional development to student achievement. Although spending on professional development may not be an ideal indicator of quality, it does provide some insight into a school's investments in building staff capacity, and its effect should be assessed analytically.

School and Class Size

Research on the impact of school size on student achievement is clearer than research on class size; the optimum size for elementary schools is 300 to 500, and the optimum size for secondary schools is 600 to 900 (Lee & Smith, 1997; Raywid, 1997–1998). Given the current stock of large school buildings, this means creating several independent schools within these larger buildings, each with a separate student body, separate principal, and separate entrance. Thus, it would be important to include some measure of total school size as well as size of "schools within schools," if they exist.

The effect of class size on student achievement has been one of the most extensively researched elements of school resources over the past decade due to the high level of policy interest surrounding it as well as the opportunities for experimental design—something rare in education research. Effect sizes of small classes (generally defined as fewer than 20 students per class) have ranged from 0.1 to 0.4 *SD*s depending on grade level (Finn, 2002; Grissmer, 2001; Hedges & Greenwald, 1996). The research also suggests that the effects of smaller classes persist into later grades and are particularly beneficial to poor and minority students (Finn, Gerger, Achilles, & Zaharias, 2001; Nye, Hedges, & Konstantopulos, 2001a, 2001b).

The well-known, randomized, Project Star class-size study in Tennessee (Folger, 1992) examined the effect of smaller classes of 15 on more than 12,000 students over 4 years. Among the findings of the Star study were that small classes in Kindergarten through Grade 3 increased achievement across school subjects by 0.2 to 0.3 *SD*s and perhaps as importantly substantially reduced the achievement gap between White and minority students. Consistent positive effects have also been found in studies of class size initiatives in Wisconsin, North Carolina, and California (Finn, 2002).

Schools could also organize the school day so that small classes are provided for just some subjects such as reading and math. These class size approaches could also be studied.

Summary

In sum, research has shown so far that the following key school factors are linked to student learning gains:

1. Principal instructional leadership.
2. School culture, both high expectations and a professional culture.
3. Nature of and level of investment in effective professional development.
4. School and class size.

Other school variables could also emerge and become variables to include in a comprehensive student-, classroom-, and school-level educational model.

Student Effects

Actions or dispositions of individual students also impact their own learning. There is a long tradition of psychological and sociological work showing that various forms of both human agency and social stratification affect students' educational and occupational outcomes. Social cognitive theory, for instance, suggests that behaviors are not determined autonomously by individuals and are not dictated by environmental forces alone (Bandura, 1986). Motivation and action are instead developed within an interactive system of individual action, cognition, affect, and environmental events. This perspective is also consistent with the achievement motivation literature, which tends to show not only that academic success is ascribed to high ability and effort and failure is attributed to low ability and effort but also that expectancies for success change as a result of environmental factors. Student engagement in school also impacts learning (Finn, 1993; Marks, 2000; Newmann, 1992), although this research tradition has not been able to disentangle general school engagement from active engagement in the learning process, the latter of which would be hypothesized to have a large impact on learning. The identification of environmental factors operating at the individual level is also fundamental to much of the sociological literature. One of the most storied theories from this tradition is the Wisconsin model (Alexander, Eckland, & Griffin, 1975; Sewell, Haller, & Portes, 1969; Sewell & Hauser, 1975). This model of educational and occupational attainment posits that educational aptitude, expectations, and aspirations affect school and career outcomes. In addition, however, this work cites social resources in the form of parental education, parental occupational status, and family income as having key stratifying influences in students' school and career successes. Following in the sociological tradition of stratification, other streams of research have identified race/ethnicity in addition to socioeconomic status as a factor that shapes students' educational trajectories (Jencks & Phillips, 1998).

Prior ability, achievement motivation, effort, socioeconomic, racial/ethnic, and other family background characteristics are central to understanding individual-level effects on student achievement outcomes. Taken together, this research also stresses the importance of couching individual behaviors, affect, and outcomes within the environmental context. Empirical analysis of the classroom and school factors that may influence individuals and that may mediate the connections between such student-level variables and school outcomes have not been explored sufficiently, however.

Other Research on Teacher and School Effects

Another research tradition contributing to our predictions about school and classroom effects derives from production functions conducted largely by economists. In most of these studies, researchers have sought to predict a *school output*, most often defined as student scores on standardized tests as a function of school inputs and student and school demographic characteristics (Picus, 2001). The findings from such studies have been mixed, with earlier studies having shown school inputs had little or no effect on student achievement (Coleman et al., 1966; Hanushek, 1986; Jencks et al., 1972) and some later studies having shown mild but positive effects (Hedges, Laine, & Greenwald, 1994; Krueger, 1999). These studies found, on average, that differences in school resources accounted for only 5% to

9% of total variation in student achievement (Reynolds, Teddlie, Creemer, Scheerens, & Townsend, 2000).

One of the earliest and most influential production function studies, The Coleman Report (Coleman et al., 1966), found minimal school resource effects on student achievement. This study concluded that a student's socioeconomic background, rather than school attributes, accounted for the majority of variation in achievement. The study found that socioeconomic status accounted for more than 70% of the variation in student achievement, whereas schools and teachers accounted for only 10% to 20% of the variation.

A number of later production function studies seemed to have confirmed Coleman et al.'s (1966) findings that *school resources,* defined as direct inputs such as per-pupil expenditures, teacher salaries, or teacher experience and educational attainment, have had little effect on student learning (Hanushek, 1986, 1989, 1996, p. 27; Jencks et al., 1972). In most of these studies, however, variables have been measured at the district level, so both school and teacher variables were district averages of those variables rather than measures of those variables at the individual school or teacher level. Hanushek (1986) concluded that although dramatic differences in the effectiveness of schools and teachers could be found, there appeared to be no systematic relationships between educational expenditures and student performance. In a later review of production function research, Hanushek (1996) found that the factors behind variations in spending per pupil, such as teacher–pupil ratio, teacher education level, and teacher experience, were not consistently related to student outcomes.

However, Hanushek (1986) acknowledged that the negative results of this research could be the result of a misspecification of the production function models. In most cases, the characteristics of schools and teachers included in these studies have consisted of readily available data such as per-pupil expenditures, class size, and teacher background and experience. If these factors were not the most important in determining student performance, then the effects of schools and teachers would have been underestimated. We add to this caveat that if the school and teacher variables were aggregated to district averages, much of their variation across students would be eliminated, thus reducing the ability to find a statistical linkage.

Another well-known meta-analysis of production function studies (Greenwald, Hedges, & Laine, 1996) found that variations in school resources such as per-pupil spending, teacher salaries, and other teacher background characteristics were significantly associated with student achievement levels, so much so that the researchers suggested that "moderate increases in spending may be associated with significant increases in achievement" (p. 362). A study by Card and Krueger (1992) found that men educated in higher quality schools (measured in terms of pupil–teacher ratio, length of school year, and teacher salaries) had higher career earnings (an alternative measure of school output).

For the purposes of this article, the production function research is not all that helpful. Some studies have supported some of the variables we identified in the previous sections, and other studies have not. However, because most of the studies use district-level variables, their findings cannot be considered conclusive. Even the production function studies with school-level variables could provide important information on school factors but not on teacher variables aggregated up to school-level averages.

Another and relatively newer set of research studies is that being conducted by labor market economists. For the most part, these studies have used large databases with information on individual teachers as well as student achievement. The studies have supported several of the teacher characteristic variables discussed previously such as verbal ability (Ehrenberg & Brewer, 1995), ACT scores (Ferguson & Ladd, 1996), quality of college or university attended (Ehrenberg & Brewer, 1994; Summers & Wolfe, 1975), and mathematics or science major for secondary teachers (Goldhaber & Brewer, 1997; Monk & King, 1994; Rowan et al., 1997). The studies have produced mixed results on the impact of teacher licensure (most studies have been indeterminate or mixed, e.g., Goldhaber & Brewer, 1999, 2000; Hanushek, 1992; Murnane, 1975; Murnane & Phillips, 1981; Summers and Wolfe, 1975, 1977; and the determinate findings were both positive, e.g., Ferguson & Ladd, 1996, and negative, e.g., Ehrenberg & Brewer, 1994). One of the most important contributions of these studies has been to show that teachers generally but specifically secondary teachers and secondary teachers in technical areas (mathematics, physics, biology, computers, etc.) are paid below what they need to be paid in terms of labor market benchmarking (Goldhaber, 2001; Goldhaber & Player, 2003). Finally, Ballou and Podgursky (1997) showed that increasing teacher salaries via the single salary schedule was an ineffective strategy for raising teacher quality, concluding that some type of performance pay structure was needed to ensure that the largest increases were provided to the most effective teachers.

Multilevel Educational Model

The overall goal of research over time would be to estimate the effect of a particular variable as one of several variables included in a comprehensive analytical and nested educational model of school, classroom, and student variables that included the ones described in previous sections. All variables in the comprehensive model should be specified within a multi-level analytical framework. Although we know that not all studies will be able to include all variables, our hope would be that each study would include at least some key school, classroom, and student variables so that effects of each level and individual variables over time would emerge from an integrated, multilevel analysis. The general model is summarized in Figure 1.

HLM is particularly well suited for analyzing the variables in the model because it takes into account the nested nature of the data in which students are nested within classrooms and classrooms within schools. With HLM, variation in student achievement can be explained as a function of classroom and/or school characteristics while still taking into account variance within classrooms or schools at the student level. It can also estimate between- and within-group (e.g., within and between classrooms) variance at the same time, making for more precise estimates of school and classroom effects (Arnold, 1992; Raudenbush & Bryk, 2002).

Student test scores on a standardized assessment for at least 2 consecutive years would be used in an HLM to derive a value-added measure of student achievement using Year 1 test scores to control for prior learning for each school and each teacher within schools. Of course, data for more than 2 years would permit development of longitudinal student achievement growth trajectories, which would have the potential to provide even better estimates of student learning over time. Such a model can be used to decompose the portion of total variation in student test scores that is attributable to students, teachers, and schools.

Value-added measures of school and teacher performance would be used because they effectively "isolate statistically the contribution of schools (and teachers) from other sources of student achievement" (Meyer, 1996, p. 200) such as family, student, or community characteristics or prior instruction in other schools or classrooms. Meyer (1996) pointed out that the average test score, perhaps the most commonly used school performance indicator, is seriously flawed. First, the average test score reflects all of the learning that has

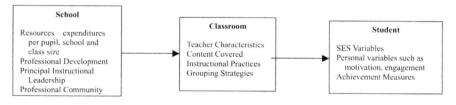

Figure 1. Comprehensive educational model of school and classroom effects on student learning gains.

21

taken place for a child prior to the test rather than only during the time period of interest (e.g., the past school year). They also reflect the effects of other schools or classrooms in which the child has been enrolled. Finally, average test scores are also confounded with the average effects of student, family, and community characteristics such as poverty (Meyer, 1996).

The conventional value-added HLM model can be shown as follows (Heistad, 1999; Meyer, 1996):

$$\text{Posttest}_{ics} = \gamma + \theta \text{Pretest}_{ics} + \alpha \text{StudChar}_{ics} + \eta_{cs} + \varepsilon_{ics},$$

where γ is a constant, θ and α are model parameters for student pretest scores and student/family characteristics, η is the teacher effect to be estimated, i indexes individual students, c indexes teachers, and s indexes schools.

A full educational model could help us begin to explore the extent to which school-level expenditures explain students' school outcomes above and beyond student and teacher-level effects. In addition, this HLM could tell researchers whether certain key school-level expenditures moderate teacher effects on student outcomes. For instance, in a three-level model with students at Level 1, classrooms at Level 2, and schools at Level 3, we could examine the impacts of school-level expenditures on the within-school mean teacher effects and on within-school teacher slopes, that is, on the variation of individual teacher effects within a school.

This specification begins with a value-added estimate of students' achievement outcomes at Level 1 of the analytical model. At Level 2, teacher characteristics are used to explain between-classroom variation in the value-added outcomes. Finally, at Level 3 of the model, school-specific expenditure data are used as predictors of school-to-school differences in value-added achievement outcomes and as cross-level interactions with teacher characteristics. We describe a specific example of how such a model may help us more clearly examine the effects of school-level expenditures in the educational model next.

Level 1: Individual Student Value-Added Outcomes

At Level 1, each student's spring test score is predicted by the previous spring's test score and individual background characteristics. The linear model for this level of the analysis is written as

$$Y_{ics} = \beta_{0cs} + \beta_{1cs}(\text{Pretest})_{ics} + \beta_{2cs}(\text{StudChar})_{ics} + r_{ics},$$

where Y_{ics} is the outcome for person i in classroom c from school j, β_{1cs}(Pretest)$_{ics}$ is the coefficient for pretest regressed on posttest, β_{2cs}(StudChar)$_{ics}$ is the coefficient for student characteristics regressed on posttest, and r_{ics} is a student-specific residual. The coefficients have subscripts i, c, and s because they are person specific, that is, each person i in classroom c and school j may have different values of these parameters.

Level 2: Model of Classroom Effects

The student achievement intercept and slopes become the outcome variables in the Level 2 models in which they are assumed to vary across classrooms within schools. With a measure of teachers' years of experience as a predictor, the Level 2 model for the achievement intercept is

$$\beta_{0cs} = \gamma_{00} + \gamma_{01}W(\text{YearsExp})_{cs} + U_{0cs},$$

where the value-added achievement level in classroom c within school s, β_{0cs}, is predicted by a classroom intercept, a teacher-specific years of experience measure, $\gamma_{01}W(\text{YearsExp})_{cs}$, and a teacher-specific residual, U_{0cs}.

Level 3: Model of School Effects

At Level 3 it is possible to predict the variation in classroom mean achievement intercepts and slopes with school-level expenditure data. The basic model for school s is written as

$$\gamma_{00s} = \xi_{000} + \xi_{001}Z(\text{ProfDevExp})_s + V_{00s},$$

where the average value-added achievement level for school s, γ_{00s}, is predicted by the level of professional development expenditures made by each school, $\xi_{001}Z(\text{ProfDevExp})_s$, plus a school-specific error term, V_{00s}.

It is also noteworthy that the slope or relation between teachers' years of experience and student outcomes may be modeled as an outcome to be explained by school-level professional development expenditures. That is, assuming a positive relation between greater years of experience and achievement, could added school-level professional development expenditures attenuate this relation? For instance, could investments in high-quality targeted professional development to help inexperienced teachers acquire better pedagogical skills help these teachers promote achievement levels that were equivalent to those of their more experienced colleagues? If so, the teacher-experience/achievement slopes within these schools would essentially be flat. This model and others like it could tell us how money may affect teaching and learning and therefore, how school-level differences in expenditures can make a difference.

The preceding model would be the goal for various studies. Of course, not every study will be able to include a full array of student-, classroom- and school-level variables. However, to ensure that each level is represented, some variables at each level, if only a random effects variable, should be included. Another problem faced by many studies particularly in trying to estimate school effects will be a sufficient number of schools. If the data base derives from a district, the small numbers of schools, even if they total 50 or so, will make it difficult to develop sufficient statistical power for a highly specified school-level model. In this case, a three-level effort might have to reduce itself to a two-level analysis, merging school and classroom variables (see Fermanich, 2003). Sample size can only be enhanced with larger databases, but too often large databases have excluded many of the important variables or have only crude measures of them.

Linkage to Resource Levels, Allocation, and Use

Although the connection between the proposed research, investments in education, and school finance adequacy might not be readily apparent, we provide a few examples here about how such connections could be developed. Clearly, positive findings on school and classroom size would provide evidence for the most effective size of school buildings and classrooms. If studies consistently produced statistically significant results for classes of 15 at certain grade levels or in specific subjects, there would be an evidence-based argument for investments in such small classes. If studies consistently indicated that smaller schools were more effective, there would be even more evidence than now exists to support the building of smaller buildings and hopefully the end of constructing large schools, particularly large high schools.

Similarly, the preceding research could begin to amass evidence that large ($3,000 to $5,000 per teacher per year) investments in professional development with specific program parameters—for example, longer duration, involving all faculty in a school, with sufficient coaching for classroom implementation—is worthwhile. Over time, even the appropriate level of investment could be indicated.

If future research continues to show that performance-based teacher evaluation systems are valid—that higher evaluation scores are linked to greater amounts of learning gains—there would be stronger reasons for using the results in more comprehensive knowledge and skills-based teacher salary structures such as those being developed in Cincinnati, Philadelphia, and Steamboat Springs, Colorado (Odden, 2003). Such a salary structure would pay teachers who produced more student learning a higher salary.

In addition, if research could begin to document the types of specific instructional practices in different subject areas in different grades that produce greater student learning, those instructional practices could be incorporated into effective professional development programs as well as performance evaluation systems.

Finally, if a school district or state tried a new program, and some schools/students participated and others did not, a comprehensive analysis such as proposed previously could isolate the impact of the program and determine whether it had a positive, negative, or neutral impact, thus providing hard evidence for retaining or dropping the program. If program involvement were randomly assigned, research findings on program impact would be even stronger.

In sum, research using the educational model proposed in this article and analyzed via HLM techniques could produce substantial and solid findings about the impacts on student achievement of many, many factors at the school, classroom, and student level. This is really the type of evidence-based practice and management that the new federal No Child Left Behind program calls for. Because many of the factors studied require dollar resources, the result could also provide information on where best to invest scarce educational resources and ultimately how much money would be needed to adequately education a student to state performance standards.

References

Alexander, K. L., Eckland, B. K., & Griffin, L. J. (1975). The Wisconsin model of socioeconomic achievement: A replication. *American Journal of Sociology, 81,* 324–342.

Arnold, C. (1992). An introduction to hierarchical linear models. *Measurement and Evaluation in Counseling and Development, 25*(2), 58–90.

Ballou, D., & Podgursky, M. (1997). *Teacher pay and teacher quality.* Kalamazoo, MI: W. E. Upjohn Institute for Employment Research.

Bandura, A. (1986). *Social foundations of thought and action: A social cognitive theory.* Englewood Cliffs, NJ: Prentice Hall.

Bossert, S., Dwyer, D., Rowan, B., & Lee, G. (1982). The instructional management role of the principal. *Educational Administration Quarterly, 18,* 34–64.

Bransford, J. D., Brown, A. L., & Cocking, R. R. E. (1999). *How people learn: Brain, mind, experience, and school.* Washington, DC: National Academy Press.

Brookover, W. C., Brady, C., & Flood, P. (1979). *School systems and student achievement: Schools can make a difference.* New York: Praeger.

Brophy, J., & Good, T. L. (1986). Teacher behavior and student achievement. In M. C. Wittrock (Ed.), *Handbook of research on teaching* (3rd ed., pp. 328–375). New York: Macmillan.

Bruer, J. T. (1993). *Schools for thought.* Cambridge, MA: MIT Press.

Bryk, A. S., & Raudenbush, S. W. (1988). Toward a more appropriate conceptualization of research on school effects: A three-level hierarchical linear model. *American Journal of Education, 97*, 65–108.

Burstein, L. (1980). The analysis of multi-level data in educational research and evaluation. *Review of Research in Education, 8*, 158–233.

Canady, R., & Rettig, M. (1996). *Block scheduling: A catalyst for change in high schools.* Princeton, NJ: Eye on Education, Inc.

Card, D., & Krueger, A. B. (1992). Does school quality matter? Returns to education and the characteristics of public schools in the United States. *The Journal of Political Economy, 100,* 1–40.

Cohen, M. (1983). Instructional, management and social conditions in effective schools. In A. Odden & L. D. Webb (Eds.), *School finance and school improvement linkages for the 1980s* (pp. 17–50). Cambridge, MA: Ballinger.

Coleman, J. S., Campbell, E., Hobson, C., McPartland, J., Mood, A., Weinfeld, R., et al. (1966). *Equality of educational opportunity.* Washington, DC: U.S. Government Printing Office.

Corcoran, T. B. (1995). *Helping teachers teach well: Transforming professional development* (Report No. RB–16–June 1995). Philadelphia: Consortium for Policy Research in Education.

Danielson, C. (1996). *Enhancing professional practice: A framework for teaching.* Alexandria, VA: Association for Supervision and Curriculum Development.

Darling-Hammond, L., & Youngs, P. (2002). Defining "highly qualified teachers": What does "scientifically based research" actually tell us? *Educational Researcher, 31*(9), 13–25.

Desimone, L., Porter, A. C., Birman, B. F., Garet, M. S., & Yoon, K. S. (2002). How do district management and implementation strategies relate to the quality of professional development that districts provide to teachers? *Teachers College Record 104,* 1265–1312.

Desimone, L. M., Porter, A. C., Garet, M. S., Yoon, K. S., & Birman, B. F. (2002). Effects of professional development on teachers' instruction: Results from a three-year longitudinal study. *Educational Evaluation and Policy Analysis, 24,* 81–112.

Edmonds, R. (1979). Effective schools for the urban poor. *Educational Leadership, 37*(1), 15–24.

Ehrenberg, R .G., & Brewer, D. J. (1994). Do school and teacher characteristics matter?: Evidence from high school and beyond. *Economics of Education Review, 13,* 1–17.

Ehrenberg, R. G., & Brewer, D. J. (1995). Did teachers' verbal ability and race matter in the 1960s?: *Coleman* revisited. *Economics of Education Review,14,* 1–21.

Elmore, R. F. (2002). *Bridging the gap between standards and achievement: The imperative for professional development in education.* Washington, DC: Albert Shanker Institute.

Fennema, E., & Romberg, T. (1999). *Mathematics classrooms that promote understanding.* Mahwah, NJ: Lawrence Erlbaum Associates, Inc.

Ferguson, R. F. (1991, Summer). Paying for public education: New evidence on how and why money matters. *Harvard Journal on Legislation, 28,* 465–497.

Ferguson, R. F. (1998). Teachers' perceptions and expectations and the Black–White test score gap. In C. Jencks & M. Phillips (Eds.), *The Black–White test score gap* (pp. 273–317). Washington, DC: Brookings Institute.

Ferguson, R. F., & Ladd, H. F. (1996). How and why money matters: An analysis of Alabama schools. In H.F. Ladd (Ed.), *Holding schools accountable: Performance-based reform in education* (pp. 265–298). Washington, DC: Brookings Institute.

Fermanich, M. (2002). School spending for professional development: A cross case analysis of seven schools in one urban district. *Elementary School Journal 103,* 27–50.

Fermanich, M. (2003). *School resources and student achievement: The effect of school-level resources on instructional practices and student outcomes in Minneapolis public schools.* Unpublished doctoral dissertation, University of Wisconsin–Madison.

Finn, J. (1993, August). *School engagement and students at risk* (NCES Publication No. 93470). Washington, DC: National Center for Education Research, Statistics, Research and Development Reports.

Finn, J. D. (2002). Small classes in American schools: Research, practice, and politics. *Phi Delta Kappan, 83*, 551–560.

Finn, J. D., & Achilles, C. M. (1999). Tennessee's class size study: Findings, implications, misconceptions. *Educational Evaluation and Policy Analysis, 21*, 97–110.

Finn, J. D., Gerger, S. B., Achilles, C. M., & Zaharias, J. B. (2001). The enduring effects of small classes. *Teachers College Record, 103*, 145–183.

Folger, J. (Ed.). (1992). Project STAR and class size policy [Special issue]. *Peabody Journal of Education, 67*(1).

Gallagher, H. A. (2004/this issue). Vaughn Elementary's innovative teacher evaluation system: Are teacher evaluation scores related to growth in student achievement? *Peabody Journal of Education, 79*(4), 79–107.

Gamoran, A. (1992). The variable effects of high school tracking. *American Sociological Review, 57*, 812–828.

Gamoran, A. (1993). Alternative uses of ability grouping in secondary schools: Can we bring high-quality instruction to low-ability classes? *American Journal of Education, 101*, 1–22.

Gamoran, A. (1996). Curriculum standardization and equality of opportunity in Scottish secondary education, 1984–1990. *Sociology of Education, 29*, 1–21.

Gamoran, A. (1997). Curriculum change as a reform strategy: Lessons from the United States and Scotland. *Teachers College Record, 98*, 608–628.

Gamoran, A. (1998). Differentiation and opportunity in restructured schools. *American Journal of Education, 106*, 385–415.

Gamoran, A., Porter, A. C., Smithson, J., & White, P. A. (1997). Upgrading high school mathematics instruction: Improving learning opportunities for low-income youth. *Education Evaluation and Policy Analysis, 19*, 325–338.

Garet, M., Birman, B., Porter, A. C., Yoon, K., & Desimone, L. (2002). What makes professional development effective? Analysis of a national sample of teachers. *American Education Research Journal, 38*, 915–945.

Goldhaber, D. D. (2001). How has teacher compensation changed? In W. Fowler, Jr. (Ed.), *Selected papers in school finance, 2000* (pp. 11–40). Washington, DC: U.S. Department of Education, National Center for Education Statistics.

Goldhaber, D. D. (2002). The mystery of good teaching. *Education Next, 2*(1), 50–55.

Goldhaber, D. D., & Brewer, D. J. (1997). Evaluating the effect of teacher degree level on educational performance. In W. J. Fowler (Ed.), *Developments in school finance, 1996* (pp. 197–210). Washington, DC: National Center for Education Statistics, U.S. Department of Education.

Goldhaber, D., & Brewer, D. (1999). Teacher licensing and student achievement. In M. Kanstoroom & C. E. Finn (Eds.), *Better teachers, better schools* (pp. 83–102). Washington, DC: Thomas B. Fordham Foundation.

Goldhaber, D. D., & Brewer, D. J. (2000). Does teacher certification matter? High school teacher certification status and student achievement. *Educational Evaluation and Policy Analysis, 22*, 129–145.

Goldhaber, D., & Player, D. (2003). *What different benchmarks suggest about how financially attractive it is to teach in public schools.* Madison: University of Wisconsin, Wisconsin Center for Education Research, Consortium for Policy Research in Education.

Greenwald, R., Hedges, L. V., & Laine, R. D. (1996). The effect of school resources on student achievement. *Review of Educational Research, 66*, 361–396.

Grissmer, D. (Ed.). (1999). Class size: Issues and new findings [Special issue]. *Educational Evaluation and Policy Analysis, 21*(2).

Grissmer, D. (2001). Research directions for understanding the relationship of educational resources to educational outcomes. In S. Chaikind & W. J. Fowler (Eds.), *Education finance in the new millennium* (pp. 139–155). Larchmont, NY: Eye On Education.

Hallinger, P., & Heck, R. H. (1996). Reassessing the principal's role in school effectiveness: A review of empirical research, 1980–1995. *Educational Administration Quarterly, 32*(1), 5–45.

Hallinger, P., & Heck, R. H. (1998). Exploring the principal's contribution to school effectiveness: 1980–1995. *School Effectiveness and School Improvement, 9*, 157–191.

Hanushek, E. A. (1986). The economics of schooling: Production and efficiency in public schools. *Journal of Economic Literature, 24*, 1141–1177.

Hanushek, E. A. (1989). The impact of differential expenditures on school performance. *Educational Researcher, 18*(4), 45–65.

Hanushek, E. A. (1992). The trade-off between child quantity and quality. *Journal of Political Economy, 100*, 85–117.

Hanushek, E. A. (1996). Measuring investment in education. *Journal of Economic Perspectives, 10*(4), 9–31.

Hanushek, E. A., Kain, J. F., & Rivkin, S. G. (1998). *Teachers, schools, and academic achievement* (Working Paper No. 6691). Cambridge, MA: National Bureau of Economic Research.

Heck, R. H., Larsen, T. J., & Marcoulides, G. A. (1990). Instructional leadership and school achievement: Validation of a causal model. *Educational Administration Quarterly, 26*(2), 94–125.

Hedges, L. V., & Greenwald, R. (1996). Have times changed? The relation between school resources and student performance. In G. Burtless (Ed.), *Does money matter? The effect of school resources on student achievement and adult success* (pp. 74–92). Washington, DC: Brookings Institute.

Hedges, L. V., Laine, R. D., & Greenwald, R. (1994). Does money matter? A meta-analysis of studies of the effects of differential school inputs on student outcomes. *Educational Researcher, 23*(3), 5–14.

Heistad, D. (1999, April). *Teachers who beat the odds: Value-added reading instruction in Minneapolis 2nd grade classrooms.* Paper presented at the annual meeting of the American Educational Research Association, Montreal, Quebec, Canada.

Holtzapple, E. (2001). *Report on the validation of teachers evaluation system instructional domain ratings.* Cincinnati, OH: Cincinnati Public Schools.

Holtzapple, E. (2002, November). *Validating a teacher evaluation system.* Paper presented at the annual meeting of the American Evaluation Association, Washington, DC.

Jencks, C. S., & Mayer, S. E. (1990). The social consequences of growing up in a poor neighborhood. In L. E. Lynn & M. McGeary (Eds.), *Inner-city poverty in the United States* (pp. 111–186). Washington, DC: National Academy of Sciences.

Jencks, C. S., & Phillips, M. (1998). *The Black–White test score gap.* Washington, DC: Brookings Institute.

Jencks, C. S., Smith, M., Ackland, H., Bane, M. J., Cohen, D., Ginter, H., et al. (1972). *Inequality: A reassessment of the effect of the family and schooling in America.* New York: Basic Books.

Kimball, S. M., White, B., Milanowski, A. T., & Borman, G. (2004/this issue). Examining the relationship between teacher evaluation and student assessment results in Washoe County. *Peabody Journal of Education, 79*(4), 54–78.

Krueger, A. B. (1999). Experimental estimates of education production functions. *Quarterly Journal of Economics, 114*, 497–533.

Krueger, A. B., & Whitmore, D. M. (2001). *Would smaller classes help close the Black–White achievement gap?* (Working Paper No. 451). Princeton, NJ: Princeton University. Retrieved June 1, 2002, from http://www.irs.princeton.edu/pubs/pdfs/451.pdf

Lee, V., & Smith, J. (1997). High school size: Which works best, and for whom? *Educational Evaluation and Policy Analysis, 19,* 205–228.

Little, J. W. (1993). Teachers' professional development in a climate of education reform. *Educational Evaluation and Policy Analysis, 15,* 129–151.

Louis, K. S., & Marks, H. M. (1998). Does professional community affect the classroom? Teachers' work and student experiences in restructuring schools. *American Journal of Education, 106,* 532–575.

Marks, H. M. (2000). Student engagement in instructional activity: Patterns in the elementary, middle and high school years. *American Educational Research Journal, 37,* 153–184.

Meyer, R. H. (1996). Value-added indicators of school performance. In E. A. Hanushek & D. W. Jorgenson (Eds.), *Improving America's schools: The role of incentives* (pp. 197–223). Washington, DC: National Academy Press.

Meyer, R. H. (2001). *Estimation of teacher and school performance in the Denver public schools: A feasibility study.* Madison: University of Wisconsin–Madison, Wisconsin Center for Educational Research.

Milanowski, A. (2004/this issue). The relation between teacher performance evaluation scores and student achievement: Evidence from Cincinnati. *Peabody Journal of Education, 79*(4), 33–53.

Miles, K. H., Odden, A., Fermanich, M., Archibald, S., & Gallagher, H. A. (in press). Understanding and comparing district investment in professional development: Methods and lessons from four districts. *Journal of Education Finance.*

Minorini, P., & Sugarman, S. (1999). Educational adequacy and the courts: The promise and problems of moving to a new paradigm. In H. Ladd, R. Chalk, & J. Hansen (Eds.), *Equity and adequacy in education finance: Issues and perspectives* (pp. 175–208). Washington, DC: National Academy Press.

Monk, D. H. (1994). Subject area preparation of secondary math and science teachers and student achievement. *Economics of Education Review, 13,* 125–145.

Monk, D. H., & King, J. (1994). Multilevel teacher resource effects on pupil performance in secondary mathematics and science: The case of teacher subject-matter preparation. In R. Ehrenberg (Ed.), *Contemporary policy issues: Choices and consequences in education* (pp. 29–58). Ithaca, NY: ILR Press.

Murnane, R. J. (1975). *The impact of school resources on the learning of inner city children.* Cambridge, MA: Ballinger.

Murnane, R. J. (1983). Quantitative studies of effective schools: What have we learned? In A. Odden & L. D. Webb (Eds.), *School finance and school improvement: Linkages for the 1980's* (pp. 193–209). Cambridge, MA: Ballinger.

Murnane, R. J., & Phillips, B. R. (1981). What do effective teachers of inner-city children have in common? *Social Science Research, 10,* 83–100.

Murphy, J. (1994). Transformational change and the evolving role of the principal: Early empirical evidence. In J. Murphy & K. Seashore Louis (Eds.), *Reshaping the principalship: Insights from transformational reform efforts* (pp. 20–53). Thousand Oaks, CA: Corwin Press.

Newmann, F. (1992). *Student engagement and achievement in American secondary schools.* New York: Teachers College Press.

Newmann, F. M., & Wehlage, G. G. (1995). *Successful school restructuring: A report to the public and educators.* Madison: University of Wisconsin–Madison, Center on Organization and Restructuring of Schools.

No Child Left Behind Act of 2001, Pub. L. No. 107–110, 115 Stat. 1425. (2002).

Nye, B. A., Hedges, L. V., & Konstantopulos, S. (2001a). Are effects of small classes cumulative: Evidence from a Tennessee experiment. *The Journal of Educational Research, 94,* 336–345.

Nye, B. A., Hedges, L. V., & Konstantopulos, S. (2001b). The long-term effects of small classes in early grades: Lasting benefits in mathematics achievement at grade nine. *Journal of Experimental Education, 69,* 245–258.

Odden, A. (2003). An early assessment of comprehensive teacher compensation change plans. In D. Monk & M. Plecki (Vol. Eds.), *School finance and teacher quality: Exploring the connections. 2003 Yearbook of the American Education Finance Association* (pp. 209–228). Larchmont, NY: Eye on Education.

Odden, A., Archibald, S., Fermanich, M., & Gallagher, H. A. (2002). A cost framework for professional development. *The Journal of Education Finance, 28,* 51–74.

Pavan, B. (1992). The benefits of nongraded schools. *Educational Leadership, 50*(2), 22–25.

Picus, L. O. (2001). *In search of more productive schools: A guide to resource allocation in education.* Eugene: ERIC Clearinghouse on Educational Management, University of Oregon.

Porter, A. C. (1994). National standards and school improvement in the 1990s: Issues and promise. *American Journal of Education, 102,* 421–449.

Porter, A. C. (1998, October). *Curriculum reform and measuring what is taught: Measuring the quality of education processes.* Paper presented at the annual meeting of the Association for Public Policy Analysis and Management, New York.

Porter, A. C. (2002). Measuring the content of instruction: Uses in research and practice. *Educational Researcher, 31*(7), 3–14.

Porter, A. C., & Smithson, J. (2001). Are content standards being implemented in the classroom? A methodology and some tentative answers. In S. H. Fuhrman (Ed.), *From the capitol to the classroom: Standards-based reform in the states* (100th Yearbook of the National Science Foundation on Grant No. SPA–8953446 to the Consortium for Policy Research in Education). Madison: University of Wisconsin, Wisconsin Center for Education Research.

Purkey, S. C., & Smith, M. S. (1983). Effective schools: A review. *The Elementary School Journal, 83,* 427–452.

Raudenbush, S. W., & Bryk, A. S. (1986). A hierarchical model for studying school effects. *Sociology of Education, 59,* 1–17.

Raudenbush, S. W., & Bryk, A. S. (2002). *Hierarchical linear models: Applications and data analysis methods.* Thousand Oaks, CA: Sage.

Raywid, M. A. (1997–1998). Synthesis of research: Small schools: A reform that works. *Educational Leadership, 55*(4), 34–39.

Reynolds, D., Teddlie, C., Creemer, B., Scheerens, J., & Townsend, T. (2000). An introduction to school effectiveness research. In C. Teddlie & D. Reynolds (Eds.), *The international handbook of school effectiveness research* (pp. 3–25). London: Falmer.

Rice, J. K. (2001). Illuminating the black box: The evolving role of education productivity research. In S. Chaikind & W. J. Fowler (Eds.), *Education finance in the new millennium* (pp. 121–138). Larchmont, NY: Eye On Education.

Rivkin, S. G., Hanushek, E. A., & Kain, J. F. (2001). *Teachers, schools, and academic achievement.* Unpublished manuscript, Amherst College, Amherst, MA.

Rosenshine, B., & Stevens, R. (1986). Teaching functions. In M. C. Witrick (Ed.), *Handbook of research on teaching* (pp. 376–391). New York: Macmillan.

Rowan, B. (1999). *Assessing teacher quality: insights from school effectiveness research.* Unpublished manuscript, University of Michigan, Ann Arbor.

Rowan, B., Camburn, E., & Richard, C. (2002, March). *Using logs to measure the "enacted curriculum" in large-scale surveys: Insights from the study of instructional improvement.* Paper presented at the annual meeting of the American Educational Research Association, New Orleans, LA.

Rowan, B., Chiang, F.-S., & Miller, R. J. (1996, April). *Using research on employee performance to study teaching effectiveness: An analysis of teacher effects on student achievement in mathematics using NELS 88 Data.* Paper presented at the annual meeting of the American Educational Research Association, New York.

Rowan, B., Chiang, F.-S., & Miller, R. J. (1997). Using research on employees' performance to study the effects of teachers on students' achievement. *Sociology of Education, 70,* 256–284.

Rowan, B., Correnti, R., & Miller, R. J.(2002). What large-scale, survey research tells us about teacher effects on student achievement: Insights from the prospects study of elementary schools. *Teachers College Record, 104,* 1525–1567.

Sanders, W. L. (2000). *Value-added assessment from student achievement data.* Cary, NC: Create National Evaluation Institute.

Sanders, W. L., & Horn, S. P. (1994). The Tennessee Value-Added Assessment System (TVAAS): Mixed-model methodology in educational assessment. *Journal of Personnel Evaluation in Education, 8,* 299–311.

Sanders, W. L., & Rivers, J. C. (1996). *Cumulative and residual effects of teachers on future student academic achievement.* Knoxville: University of Tennessee Value-Added Research and Assessment Center.

Scheerens, J., Nanninga, C. R., & Pelgrum, W. J. H. (1989). Generalizability of instructional and school effectiveness indicators across nations: Preliminary results of a secondary analysis of the IEA Second Mathematics Study. In B. Creemer, T. Peters, & D. Reynolds (Eds.), *Proceedings of the Second International Congress, Rotterdam 1989* (pp. 199–209). Lisse, The Netherlands: Swets & Zeitinger.

Sewell, W. H., Haller, A. O., & Portes, A. (1969). The educational and early occupational attainment process. *American Sociological Review, 27,* 517–522.

Sewell, W. H., & Hauser, R. M. (1975). *Education, occupation, and earnings: Achievement in the early career.* New York: Academic.

Slavin, R. (1987). Ability grouping and student achievement in elementary schools: A best evidence synthesis. *Review of Educational Research, 57,* 293–336.

Slavin, R. (1992). The nongraded elementary school: Great potential but keep it simple. *Educational Leadership, 50*(2), 24–25.

Slavin, R., & Karweit, N. (1985). Effects of whole class, ability grouped and individualized instruction on mathematics achievement. *American Educational Research Journal, 22,* 351–357.

Smith, J. B., Lee, V. E., & Newmann, F. M. (2001). *Instruction and achievement in Chicago elementary schools.* Report of the Chicago Annenberg Research Project. Chicago: Consortium on Chicago School Research. (Available from http://www.consortium-chicago.org/publications/pdfs/p0f01.pdf)

Smylie, M. (1996). From bureaucratic control to building human capital: The importance of teacher learning in education reform. *Educational Researcher, 25*(9), 9–11.

Sorenson, A., & Hallinan, M. (1977). A reconceptualization of school effects. *Sociology of Education, 50,* 273–289.

Sparks, D., & Hirsh, S. (1999). *A national plan for improving professional development* (National Staff Development Council report). Oxford, OH: National Staff Development Council. (Available from http://www.nsdc.org/library/authors/NSDCPlan.cfm)

Stigler, J., & Hiebert, J. (1999) *The teaching gap: Best ideas from the world's teachers for improving education in the classroom.* New York: Free Press.

Summers, A. A., & Wolfe, B. L. (1975). *Equality of educational opportunity qualified: A production function approach* (Research Paper No. 6). Philadelphia: Federal Reserve Bank of Philadelphia, Department of Research.

31

Summers, A. A., & Wolfe, B. L (1977). Do schools make a difference? *American Economic Review, 67*, 639–652.

Veenman, S. (1995). Cognitive and noncognitive effects of multigrade and multi-age classes: A best evidence synthesis. *Review of Educational Research, 65*, 319–381.

Wayne, A. J., & Youngs, P. (2003). Teacher characteristics and student achievement gains: A review. *Review of Educational Research, 73*, 89–122.

Webster, W. J., Mendro, R. L., Orsak, T. H., & Weerasinghe, D. (1996, April). *The applicability of selected regression and hierarchical linear models to the estimation of school and teacher effects.* Paper presented at the annual meeting of the National Council on Measurement in Education, New York.

Webster, W. J., Mendro., R. L., Orsak, T. H., & Weerasinghe, D. (1998, April). *An application of hierarchical linear modeling to the estimation of school and teacher effect.* Paper presented at the annual meeting of the American Educational Research Association, San Diego, CA.

Wright, P. S., Horn, S. P., & Sanders, W. L. (1997). Teacher and classroom context effects on student achievement: Implications for teacher evaluation. *Journal of Personnel Evaluation in Education, 11*, 57–67.

PEABODY JOURNAL OF EDUCATION, 79(4), 33–53

The Relationship Between Teacher Performance Evaluation Scores and Student Achievement: Evidence From Cincinnati

Anthony Milanowski
Consortium for Policy Research in Education
University of Wisconsin–Madison

In this article, I present the results of an analysis of the relationship between teacher evaluation scores and student achievement on district and state tests in reading, mathematics, and science in a large Midwestern U.S. school dis-

Some portions of this article were presented at the 2003 annual meeting of the American Educational Research Association, Chicago on April 21. Since that time, some additional data have been collected and some results have changed. The research reported herein was supported in part by a grant from the U.S. Department of Education, Office of Educational Research and Improvement, National Institute on Educational Governance, Finance, Policymaking, and Management to the Consortium for Policy Research in Education (CPRE) and the Wisconsin Center for Education Research, School of Education, University of Wisconsin–Madison (Grant OERI–R3086A60003). The opinions expressed are those of the author and do not necessarily reflect the view of the National Institute on Educational Governance, Finance, Policymaking, and Management, Office of Educational Research and Improvement, U.S. Department of Education; the institutional partners of CPRE; or the Wisconsin Center for Education Research.

I thank Dr. Elizabeth Holtzapple, Director of Research, Evaluation, and Test Administration for the Cincinnati Public Schools, for her help in obtaining and interpreting the data used in this article.

Requests for reprints should be sent to Anthony Milanowski, University of Wisconsin–Madison, Consortium for Policy Research in Education, 1025 West Johnson Street, Madison, WI 53706. E-mail: amilanow@facstaff.wisc.edu

trict. Within a value-added framework, I correlated the difference between predicted and actual student achievement in science, mathematics, and reading for students in Grades 3 through 8 with teacher evaluation ratings. Small to moderate positive correlationships were found for most grades in each subject tested. When these correlationships were combined across grades within subjects, the average correlationships were .27 for science, .32 for reading, and .43 for mathematics. These results show that scores from a rigorous teacher evaluation system can be substantially related to student achievement and provide criterion-related validity evidence for the use of the performance evaluation scores as the basis for a performance-based pay system or other decisions with consequences for teachers.

The literature reviewed by Odden, Borman, and Fermanich (2004/this issue) has suggested that teachers have substantial impacts on student learning and that teacher classroom practices are likely to be an important pathway for these effects. Odden et al. (2004/this issue) proposed that the scores from well-designed, performance-based teacher evaluation systems may provide a measure of important teacher behaviors that can be used in a comprehensive model of teacher, classroom, and school effects on student achievement. In this article, I provide evidence for the potential usefulness of such scores by examining the relationship between teacher evaluation scores in a school district with a rigorous, standards-based teacher evaluation system and a value-added measure of student achievement. The existence of a positive, substantial, and statistically significant relationship would be evidence that certain teacher behaviors have important impacts on student learning. This relationship would also provide evidence of the validity of these scores as the basis for administrative decisions with consequences for teachers.

Standards-Based Teacher Evaluation

It may seem unusual to think of teacher evaluation systems as a source of information on teacher instructional behavior that affects student learning. As a measurement process, the reputation of teacher evaluation is not particularly good. For example, Peterson (2000) concluded from his review of the literature that typical teacher evaluation practices neither improve teachers nor accurately represent what happens in the classroom. Darling-Hammond, Wise, and Pease (1983) characterized teacher evaluation methods as generally of low reliability and validity. Others have criticized teacher evaluation as superficial (Stiggens & Duke, 1988) or as based on simplistic criteria with minimal relevance to what teachers need to do to enhance student learning (Danielson & McGreal, 2000). Medley and Coker (1987) reviewed studies from the 1950s to 1970s and concluded that the relationship between principal ratings of teacher performance and student achievement was generally weak. Their own study found correlationships between principal performance ratings and learning gains of .10 to .23.

In the 1990s, an interest in making teacher assessment more performance based and reflective of a more complex conception of teaching guided the development of more sophisticated teaching assessment systems including those used by the National Board for Professional Teaching Standards and the PRAXIS III licensure assessment (Porter, Youngs, & Odden, 2001). At the school district level, a related strategy based on explicit and detailed standards for teacher performance that try to capture the content of quality instruction has attracted interest. Consistent with the movement for standards for students, this approach has been called *standards-based teacher evaluation*. Danielson and McGreal (2000) described a comprehensive approach to standards-based evaluation. It starts with a comprehensive model or description of teacher performance reflecting the current consensus on good teaching and translates this into explicit standards and multiple levels of performance defined by detailed behavioral rating scales. It also requires more intensive collection of evidence including frequent observations of classroom practice and use of artifacts such as lesson plans and samples of student work to provide a richer picture of teacher performance. One set of standards on which several district-level evaluation systems have been based is the Framework for Teaching (Danielson, 1996). According to Danielson, the Framework was intended to reflect current views of "best practice" in instruction, a pedagogical model including insights from both effective teaching research and from constructivist/authentic approaches. The higher levels of performance in this model describe teaching practice that is active, consistent with curriculum standards, differentiated, inclusive, engages students, aims at developing a community of learners, and incorporates teacher reflection. Teaching in this way is assumed to lead to higher levels of student achievement.

Standards-based teacher evaluation systems based on the Framework for Teaching would appear to have the potential to provide measurements of teacher practice that would be more strongly related to student learning. One jurisdiction that has implemented standards-based evaluation is the Cincinnati Public School District. As described next, the district developed a standards-based teacher assessment system as the foundation for both teacher evaluation and knowledge and skill-based pay. In this article, I provide a brief description of the Cincinnati evaluation system, set out a conceptual framework for the assessment of the validity of inferences based on evaluation scores for use in making decisions about teachers or as measures of teacher behaviors, and then present the results of an analysis of the relationship between teacher evaluation scores and measures of student achievement.

Performance Evaluation System in Cincinnati

Cincinnati Public Schools (CPS) is a large urban district with 48,000 students and 3,000 teachers in more than 70 schools and programs. Its average level of student achievement is low compared to the surrounding suburban districts, and a high proportion of the students are eligible for free or reduced-price lunch. CPS has also had a history of school reform activity, including the introduction of new whole-school designs (e.g., Success for All), school-based budgeting, and teams to run schools and deliver instruction. The union–management relationship has generally been positive. Teachers have generally been paid more than in surrounding districts, giving the potential to attract better teachers. Like many other urban districts, state accountability programs and public expectations have put pressure on the district to raise average student test scores.

In response to state-level changes in teacher licensing requirements, the obsolescence of the existing teacher performance evaluation system, and ambitious goals for improving student achievement, the District designed a knowledge and skill-based pay system and new teacher evaluation system during the 1998–99 school year. (See Kellor & Odden, 2000, for a description of the design process.) Both were based on a teacher performance assessment process that I describe next. The assessment system was piloted in the 1999–2000 school year and was used for teacher evaluation district wide in the 2000–01, 2001–02, and 2002–03 school years. An assessment of teacher reactions to the pilot was done by Milanowski and Heneman (2001).

The assessment system was based on a set of teaching standards derived from the Framework for Teaching (Danielson, 1996). Sixteen (later 17) performance standards were grouped into four domains: planning and preparation (Domain 1), creating an environment for learning (Domain 2), teaching for learning (Domain 3), and professionalism (Domain 4). For each standard, a set of behaviorally anchored rating scales called rubrics described four levels of performance (unsatisfactory, basic, proficient, and distinguished). Teachers were evaluated using the rubrics based on two major sources of evidence: six classroom observations and a portfolio prepared by the teacher. Four classroom observations were made by a teacher evaluator hired from the ranks of the teaching force and released from classroom teaching for 3 years. Building administrators (principals and assistant principals) did the other two observations. The portfolio included artifacts such as lesson and unit plans, attendance records, student work, family contact logs, and documentation of professional development activities. Based on summaries of the six observations, teacher evaluators made a final summative rating on each of the standards in Domains 2 and 3, whereas building administrators rated on the standards in Domains 1 and 4, primarily based on the teacher portfolio. Standard-level ratings were then aggregated to a domain-level score for each of the four domains. The full assessment system was used for a comprehensive evaluation of teachers in their 1st and 3rd years and every 5 years thereafter. A less intensive annual assessment was done in all other years, conducted only by building administrators and based on more limited evidence. The annual assessment was intended to be both an opportunity for teacher professional development and an evaluation for accountability purposes.

Both teachers and evaluators received considerable training on the new system. Evaluators were trained using a calibration process that involved rating taped lessons using the rubrics and then comparing ratings with expert judges and discussing differences. To ensure consistency among evaluators, the district eventually required that all evaluators, including principals, meet a standard of agreement with a set of reference or expert evaluators in rating videotaped lessons. Only those who met the standard were to be allowed to evaluate after the 2001–02 school year.

The performance evaluation system was designed in part to provide the foundation for the knowledge and skill-based pay system (Odden & Kelley, 2001). This system defined career levels for teachers with pay differentiated by level. The new pay system was originally scheduled to come into effect in the 2002–03 school year, resulting in relatively high stakes for many of the district's teachers. However, the link between the evaluation system and the pay system was voted down by teachers in a special election held in May 2002. The evaluation system has continued to be used for new teachers and some veterans. For beginning teachers (those evaluated in their 1st or 3rd years), the consequences of a poor comprehensive evaluation could be termination. For tenured teachers, the consequences of a positive evaluation could include eligibility for the step increases at some levels and eligibility to become a lead teacher. A poor evaluation could lead to placement in the peer assistance program and eventual termination.

Conceptual Framework for Inferences
About Teacher Evaluation Scores

Figure 1 helps explicate the use of empirical evidence of a relationship between teacher evaluation scores and measurements of student achieve-

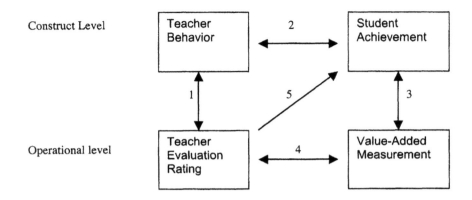

Figure 1. Inferential relationships involving use of evaluation scores in research and practice. *Note.* Adapted from *Research in Organizational Behavior* (Vol. 2), by B. M. Staw and L. L. Cummings (Eds.), 1980, Greenwich, CT: JAI. Copyright 1980 by Elsevier.

ment to support the use of the scores for administrative purposes and for research on teacher effects on student learning. The figure (see Schwab, 1980; see also Binning & Barrett, 1989) distinguishes between the construct level at which the relevant attributes or characteristics of teachers and students are represented and the operational level at which the measurements of these constructs are represented.

The figure shows five linkages:

1. The relationship between the evaluation scores and the teacher behaviors or performance they represent.
2. The theorized causal relationship between teacher behaviors and student achievement.
3. The relationship between student achievement and value-added measurements based on test scores.
4. The empirical relationship between evaluation scores and the value-added measurements.
5. The inference that differences in teachers' evaluation scores are related to differences in student learning.

Linkages 1 and 3 can be thought of as the construct validity of the measurements that represent the constructs.

District administrators intending to use teacher evaluation scores for making decisions with consequences for teachers are primarily interested in "validating" the evaluation scores.[1] They want to be justified in inferring that teachers with high scores are better *performers,* defined as producing more student learning (inference in Linkage 5). Evidence for the validity of this inference would be provided by a substantial empirical relationship between performance scores and the value-added measurements of student achievement (Linkage 4) assuming that the value-added measurements adequately represent student learning (Linkage 3). The latter link, the construct validity of the value added measurements as representations of student learning, is more or less taken as given or as trivial because test scores are typically defined by accountability systems or external constituencies as the important indicators of student learning and because many districts face considerable pressure to raise test scores from state or Federal accountability systems. In this context, Linkage 4 provides what is often called criterion-related validity evidence, so called because one performance measure (student achievement) is thought of as of closer to the ultimate goal of the organization and so considered the criterion by which the measurements to be validated are judged (see Messick, 1989). To the extent that teacher evaluation scores are empirically related to measures of student achievement, and thus, the scores distinguish between teachers who help produce more or less student achievement, district administrators have evidence to justify their inference that some teachers are better performers than others and for the use of the scores to make decisions affecting teachers. Note that in this use of teacher evaluation scores, Linkage 1 is not of primary concern once the decision has been made to adopt a particular teacher evaluation system.

Researchers interested in measuring school, classroom, and teacher effects on student learning are also interested in Linkage 4, the empirical relationship between evaluation scores and value-added measurements of student achievement. However, for them the importance of this relationship is that it provides evidence for the existence and magnitude of a causal effect of teacher behavior on student learning. In this case, the adequacy of the scores as representations of teacher behavior and of value-

---

[1]In Cincinnati, given the substantial investment in the performance assessment system and the potential further investment in higher pay for teachers rated more competent, district leaders wanted to know whether teachers who were evaluated at higher levels contributed more to the district's strategic goal of improved student achievement. An initial analysis done by the district (Holtzapple, 2002) provided evidence that the evaluation scores were related to student achievement. In that analysis, residuals from bivariate ordinary least squares (OLS) regressions of current on prior year test scores were calculated, averaged by teacher, and correlated with the sum of the four domain scores from the teacher evaluation system.

added measurements of student achievement on tests as representations of student learning, their construct validity, is also of importance. Like district administrators, researchers may judge that the value-added measurements are adequate indicators of student learning, especially in the absence of other practical candidates for this role and the policy importance of these indicators The relationship between teacher behavior and evaluation scores deserves additional consideration, however. The first issue is how well the dimensions of performance and definitions of performance levels correspond to the researcher's concept of the teacher behavior that is expected to contribute to student learning. As mentioned previously, Danielson (1996) argued that the Framework was based on both analyses of the teacher job and research on teaching effectiveness. However, a researcher planning to use teacher evaluation scores as measures of behavior needs to review the content of the model of teaching on which the evaluation system is based to judge the degree to which the system is likely to measure her or his concept of the teacher behaviors that are expected to affect student learning.

The second issue is the degree to which the judgments of the evaluators adequately represent the teacher behaviors described in the model of teaching itself. Evaluators need to be accurate in observing behaviors and translating those behaviors into scores. Although the training and calibration of evaluators, the use of multiple observations, and the use of specialized evaluators provide reasons to believe the scores of performance in Cincinnati have a degree of construct validity as representations of teacher behavior, it is important to recognize that more formal construct validity evidence would be desirable because it is possible that the evaluators may be basing their scores on some other behaviors or teacher characteristics, which may in turn also be related to student achievement. Studies aimed at providing this evidence are in progress.

In this study, I concentrated on establishing the empirical relationship between evaluation scores and value-added measures of student achievement. The analyses described following were originally intended to provide criterion-related validity evidence that the teacher evaluation scores could be used as the basis for a system of differential pay for teachers. As Figure 1 shows, this evidence is also relevant to the question of the effect of teachers' instructional practice on student learning because it represents the expected relationship at the empirical or operational level once the construct validity Linkages 1 and 3 are established. If no empirical relationship were shown, there would be little theoretical reason to pursue further the particular operationalization of teacher practice represented by this teacher evaluation system.

Method

Measures

Teacher performance scores. The comprehensive teacher evaluation scores from the system just described were obtained from the district for the 2000–01 and 2001–02 school years. Because only a subset of teachers experienced the comprehensive evaluation each year, complete evaluation scores were available for the 270 teachers who were comprehensively evaluated during the 2000–01 school year and the 335 evaluated in 2001–02. It was decided to include teachers evaluated in 2000–01 in the analyses, even though the performance criterion was the test scores of their 2001–02 students, because teacher performance was expected to be a relatively stable characteristic. Unfortunately, not all of the scores could be used in the analysis because most evaluated teachers taught subjects or grades for which no state or district standardized tests were given. Also, some teachers were excluded because they had too few students (less than three) tested in both years. Due to these exclusions, evaluation scores for only 212 teachers could be included in the analysis. (Because analyses were done separately by subject and grade, some teachers appear in two or more subject/grade analyses.)

As described previously, teachers undergoing the comprehensive evaluation received scores on four domains: planning and preparation, creating an environment for learning (classroom management), teaching for learning, and professionalism. For this analysis, the scores on the four domains were added to yield a composite evaluation score, which was taken as an overall indicator of teacher performance. (Note that the performance pay system, as designed, would have used the scores on all of the domains to determine the teacher's pay range.) The average intercorrelation between domain scores for all the teachers evaluated in 2000–01 was .60, and coefficient alpha was .86. The average intercorrelation for 2001–02 was .61, and coefficient alpha was also .86.

Teacher experience. Ideally, one would also like information on teachers' total years of experience in the field to control for experience when examining the relationship between evaluation scores and student achievement. This information was not available from the district's human resource information system, so information on teacher's years of experience with the district was provided. These data were used as a proxy for total experience, recognizing that it underestimates the experience of teachers who taught in other districts prior to employment with CPS.

Table 1

Student Achievement Measures by Grade

Grade	2001–02 Test	2000–01 Test
3	District Test	District Test
4	State Proficiency Test	District Test
5	Terra Nova	State Proficiency Test
6	State Proficiency Test	District Test
7	District Test	State Proficiency Test
8	State Proficiency Test	District Test

Student academic achievement. Student test scores for the 2001–02 school year were obtained from the district for students in Grades 3 through 8 in reading, mathematics, and science. Test scores in the same subjects from the 2000–01 school year were also obtained from the district for these subjects. Table 1 shows the tests used for each grade.

The tests are given in March of each year. They are largely multiple choice in format but most also contain some extended response items. State proficiency tests were based on state student content standards. (A set of four score ranges has been established to group students into the proficiency categories of below basic, basic, proficient, and advanced, but these were not used in this analysis.) District tests were developed by the same testing company that helped develop the state tests and are intended to cover similar content so that schools and teachers can use the results to identify students likely to have difficulties on the state test. The scores used in the analysis were the scale scores provided by the state or the test publisher rather than raw scores, percentiles, or normal curve equivalents.

It should be noted that a substantial proportion of students enrolled in each grade in 2001–02 could not be included in the analyses because either or both the 2001–02 and prior year test scores were not available or because of student mobility between schools. Only students enrolled in the school in which they were tested in March 2002 for at least 71 days prior to the test were included. In addition, students were lost from the analyses because some could not be matched with teachers, even when test scores for both years were available. This appears to be due mostly to clerical errors in the student data system. In addition, a few students were excluded from the analyses because their current or prior year scores were extreme outliers.[2] Across grades and subjects, an average of 66% of the students enrolled in

[2]These were defined as beyond the "outer fences " of the univariate distributions, or further than about two interquartile ranges from the median, or about 2.7 *SD*s from the mean of a normal distribution. See Hoaglin (1983).

March 2002 were included in the analyses. Data were available for a higher percentage of students in the lower grades in comparison with Grades 7 and 8. The Appendix shows the total numbers of students by grade, the numbers for which test scores are available, and the number of students used in the first step of the analyses described next. Comparison of the average 2001–02 test scores between the population of students tested and the group included in the analysis showed that the latter had somewhat higher test scores (an average of .12 *SDs* higher across grades and subjects) and lower variance (an average of 15% less across grades and subjects). These differences were partially due to the exclusion of students not enrolled at a school for at least 71 days and the elimination of extreme outliers, most of which represented students who obtained very low scores.

Student demographic variables. The district also provided data on several student characteristics including ethnicity, gender, receipt of free/reduced-price lunch, special education status, and days enrolled in the school. For the analyses described next, this information was used to construct a set of dummy variables for gender (female = 1), non-White (not White/Caucasian = 1), free/reduced-price lunch status (free or reduced = 1), and special education status (participation in any special education program or exemption from testing = 1). These were included as controls at Level 1 of the hierarchical linear model used to derive the average level of value added for teachers' students.

Comparing the group of students included in Step 1 of the analysis with the population of students on the district roster in March 2002 showed that the included group was somewhat more female (an average of 2.3 percentage points across grades), was more White (an average of 1.4 percentage points), was less poor (an average of 2.5 percentage points), and contained a lower proportion of special education students (an average of 2.1 percentage points). These differences did not seem large enough to indicate that the included students were not representative of the student population.

Analysis

The analyses proceeded along the lines of the value-added paradigm defining student achievement as the residual from a regression of the 2001–02 test score in a subject on the prior year's score for that subject plus other variables thought to stand for student characteristics that potentially influence student test performance. In this case, dummy variables for gender, non-White ethnicity, special education status, and receipt of free or reduced-price lunch were included as well as the number of days enrolled at the school in which testing took place.

Because of the small number of teachers in each grade for which both test score and evaluation data were available, a full multilevel analysis (i.e., with teacher evaluation scores used as a Level 2 predictor) was not done. Rather, a two-step analysis procedure was followed as outlined next. The purpose of the two-step procedure was to produce correlation coefficients that represented the relationship between teacher evaluation scores and student achievement residuals in each grade for each of the three subjects and that could be combined across grades using standard meta-analysis formulas.

The first step was intended to produce a measure or representation of the criterion—the average achievement level on the 2001–02 test for each teacher's students—controlling for prior achievement in that subject and several of the student characteristics thought to influence test scores. To do this, a two-level hierarchical linear model was estimated. The Level 1 model was

$$\text{Posttest} = B_0 + B_1 \text{ pretest} + B_2 \text{ female} + B_3 \text{ free/reduced-price lunch} + B_4 \text{ non-White} + B_5 \text{ special ed} + B_6 \text{ days enrolled in school} + R.$$

$B_0 \ldots B_6$ were within-classroom regression coefficients, and R was the Level 1 error on individual student residual. All Level 1 predictors were grand-mean centered. The Level 2 model was

$$B_{0j} = \gamma_{00} + U_{0j}.$$

At Level 2, B_{0j} represented the intercept in classroom j, γ_{00} represented the average intercept across classrooms, and U_{0j} represented the teacher-specific differences from the average of the classroom intercepts. The slopes for all Level 1 variables were treated as fixed. From this model, the empirical Bayes (EB) intercept residuals were obtained. These residuals were taken as the measure of the average student performance relevant to each teacher. Given the grand-mean centering, the EB intercept residuals represented the difference for the "average" student: average in prior year test score and other characteristics at Level 1.

Step 2 involved correlating the EB intercept residuals with teacher evaluation scores. In this step, of course, correlationships could be calculated for only those teachers for which evaluation scores were available. In addition, even if a teacher had been evaluated, if the teacher's EB intercept residual was based on fewer than three students, that teacher was dropped from the analysis. On average, about 23% of teachers for whom EB intercept residuals could be calculated based on three or more students were included in the Step 2 analyses. Analyses were done by academic subject within grade. This led to some teachers being included in more than one analysis, so the correlationships calculated for each grade and subject are not truly independent. One alternative would be to combine the EB residuals for each teacher across grades and subjects in some way. However, because a substantial proportion of teachers did not teach multiple subjects or grades, it is not clear how meaningful it would be to compare teachers whose student achievement measure was based on multiple subjects with those whose measure was based on student test scores in only one subject and grade.

An analysis was also conducted that did not include the gender, ethnic, special education, and free/reduced-lunch controls at Level 1; this was a response to the argument that these characteristics should not be considered in the assessment of teacher performance. That is, teachers should produce similar learning gains for all groups of students. Although this may not be a realistic notion, there are those who believe that controlling for ethnicity or socioeconomic status sends the message that lower levels of achievement are expected for some students.

Results

Before proceeding to estimate EB intercept residuals to be correlated with teacher evaluation scores, the proportion of student test score variance within and between teachers was estimated after controlling for prior year test scores and student characteristics. Table 2 reports the proportion of current year test score variance at the teacher level and the reliabilities of the random intercepts at the teacher level. As the table shows, there was substantial test score variance at the teacher level (ranging from 6% for Grade 8 science to 28% for Grade 4 science) even after controlling for prior year test scores and the other student characteristics.

Table 2

Percentage of Test Score Variance at Teacher Level (Level 2) and Reliability of Random Intercepts Associated With Teachers After Controlling for Prior Year Test Score and Student Characteristics

	Reading		Math		Science	
Grade	% Variance at Teacher Level	Reliability	% Variance at Teacher Level	Reliability	% Variance at Teacher Level	Reliability
3					—	—
4	11	.52	27	.72	28	.74
5	14	.59	16	.63	13	.58
6	18	.65	27	.73	19	.65
7	15	.63	14	.59	16	.62
8	7	.46	10	.54	6	.42

Table 3

Correlations Between Empirical Bayes Intercept Residuals and Total TES Score, by Grade and Subject

Grade	Reading	Math	Science
3	.43 (55)	.46 (50)	—
4	.03 (35)	.37 (32)	.19 (34)
5	.45 (32)	.53 (31)	.33 (34)
6	.37 (32)	.56 (27)	.43 (31)
7	.16 (22)	.20 (22)	−.01 (16)
8	.31 (16)	.30 (20)	.16 (16)
Combined	.32	.43	.27
Standard error	.08	.08	.09
p	< .001	< .001	.003
95% confidence interval	.18–.45	.29–.55	.09–.46

Note. The number of teachers follows each correlation in parentheses. TES = teacher evaluation system.

Another preliminary analysis was done comparing the average level of student performance (as represented by the EB intercept residuals from Step 1) between the group of evaluated teachers and the other teachers in each grade and subject. Generally, the evaluated group had lower average EB intercept residuals, but the difference was typically not significant at conventional levels. Because most of the teachers evaluated in 2001–02 were new to the district, a somewhat lower level of average student achievement was expected for the evaluated group.

Table 3 shows the correlations between the EB intercept residuals and the sum of the four domain scores provided by the teacher evaluation system. As the table shows, relatively small numbers of teachers' scores were available in each subject within grade, and so few of the individual correlations were significant at conventional levels. As might be expected given the small numbers of teachers, the correlations vary considerably, ranging from a low of near 0 in Grade 4 reading and Grade 7 science to over .5 in Grades 5 and 6 math.

Because of the small numbers of teachers underlying the correlation in each grade/subject, I decided to combine the values across grades to come up with a more precise estimate of the relationship between evaluation scores and student achievement. By analogy with meta-analysis, each grade within an academic subject was treated as a separate study and the correlationships combined using the standard formulas for a random effects treatment.[3] As Table 3 shows, the combined coefficients were all positive

[3]An *r* to *z* transformation was done and a weighted average of the *z*s was calculated with the inverse of the variances as weights. Standard errors were calculated for this average and 95% confidence intervals. These values were then transformed back into correlation coefficients. See Shadish and Haddock (1994) for a description of the details of these calculations.

and of moderate size, ranging from .43 in math to .27 in science. Lower bounds on the 95% confidence intervals all exclude zero, suggesting that the population value of the coefficients is unlikely to be zero.

Although consideration was given to combining correlation coefficients across subjects, this would have been misleading. Most of the students are the same across subjects, and about one third of the teachers are responsible for instruction in all three subjects, so samples across subjects are not independent within grades. Unfortunately, it is also the case that the same teachers are not always responsible for instruction in all subjects within grades (especially at the two highest grades) so that combining the test scores from the three subjects into one index of student achievement for Step 1 of the analyses was not an attractive option. Because some students were not tested in all three subjects and because some teachers, even at the lower grades, did not provide instruction in all three subjects, the number of teachers for which EB intercept residuals for this combined measure of student achievement could be calculated would be considerably lower than most of the sample sizes reported in Table 3.

In addition to product–moment correlations, rank order correlations (Kendall's τ) between the evaluation scores and EB intercept residuals were also calculated for teachers with three or more students tested. This was done for two reasons. First, the product–moment correlation measures the degree of linear association, and in these small samples, it is hard to be sure whether the evaluation rating average student achievement relationships were linear. The Kendall coefficient represents merely the degree to which the relationship is monotonic. Second, it could be argued that the evaluation scores did not really attain an interval level of measurement. These rank order correlations are shown in Table 4.

Table 4

Rank Order Correlations (Kendall's Tau-b) Between Empirical Bayes Intercept Residuals and Total TES Score, by Grade and Subject

Grade	Reading	Math	Science
3	.33 (55)	.34 (50)	—
4	.05 (35)	.31 (32)	.16 (34)
5	.26 (32)	.39 (31)	.17 (34)
6	.27 (32)	.37 (27)	.43 (31)
7	.09 (22)	.11 (22)	.08 (16)
8	.18 (16)	.16 (20)	.13 (16)
Weighted average	.21	.30	.21

Note. The number of teachers follows each correlation in parentheses. TES = teacher evaluation system.

The pattern of coefficients is similar to that in Table 3 except for sixth- and seventh-grade math. The weighted average of the coefficients (weighted by the number of teachers on which the correlation was based in each grade) ranged from .21 in reading and science to .30 in math. Given that Kendall's tau coefficients are generally smaller in magnitude than product–moment correlations calculated from the same data, these results were basically the same in import as those using the product–moment correlations.

Partial correlations between the evaluation scores and EB intercept residuals, controlling for teacher experience and the year in which the teacher was evaluated (2000–01 or 2001–02) were also calculated. These coefficients are shown in Table 5.

Except for seventh-grade science, the partial correlations were all positive. As might be expected, many of the partial correlations were smaller than the correlations reported in Table 3. The weighted average partial correlations were fairly close in magnitude to the combined correlations shown in Table 3 except in science, in which the partial correlation was .1 lower. These results show that there was a moderate positive relationship between teacher evaluation scores and student achievement in reading and mathematics but only a weak relationship in science after controlling for teacher experience and the year evaluated.

Two additional analyses were also conducted. First, correlations between EB intercept residuals and teacher evaluation scores were calculated for teachers who had at least 11 students tested to see if the number of students tested had an effect on the correlations and to be consistent with the inclusion criterion used by Holtzapple (2002). The results (not shown) were generally similar to those reported in Table 3. The com-

Table 5

Partial Correlations Between Empirical Bayes Intercept Residuals and Total TES Score, Controlling for Years of Teacher Experience and Year Evaluated, by Grade and Subject

Grade	Reading	Math	Science
3	.35	.39	—
4	.04	.25	.11
5	.52	.43	.21
6	.50	.55	.38
7	.29	.37	−.08
8	.62	.17	.10
Weighted average	.36	.37	.17

Note. The number of teachers follows each correlation in parentheses. TES = teacher evaluation system.

bined correlations were .36 in reading (with a confidence interval of .19–.51), .49 in math (with a confidence interval of .34–62), and .24 in science (with a confidence interval of .02–.43). Second, EB intercept residuals were also calculated from a model that did not include student gender, ethnic, free/reduced lunch, and special education characteristics as Level 1 controls. Here, the combined-grade correlations between the resulting EB intercept residuals and teacher scores were all positive but were smaller than those reported in Table 3. The combined coefficients dropped to .31 in reading, .39 in math, and .24 in science. Lower bounds on the 95% confidence intervals continued to exclude zero, although the lower bound for science was only .07.

Discussion and Conclusions

These results provide evidence that the CPS teacher evaluation scores had a moderate degree of criterion-related validity. They suggest that the teacher assessment system was able to identify which teachers had students with higher than expected levels of achievement, as measured by test scores, to a degree greater than chance. This result supports the use of the assessment system as a basis for teacher evaluation and pay differentiation and for other human resource management purposes such as needs assessment for professional development or performance remediation. The results reported here were comparable to the mean correlation of .27 between performance appraisal scores and objective measures of performance in a variety of different occupations reported by Heneman (1986) based on meta-analyses of studies of this relationship, although somewhat lower than the .39 mean reported by Bommer, Johnson, Rich, Podsakoff, and MacKenzie (1995). They were larger than those reported by Medley and Coker (1987) and larger than the correlationships of .17 to .24 between total teacher evaluation scores and a measure of adjusted test score gains reported by Fritsche, Weerasinghe, and Babu (2003).

The results also suggest that teacher evaluation scores may be useful as representations of teaching practices that affect student learning. The empirical results show that evaluations produced by a relatively rigorous, standards-based system are related to an accepted measure of student learning. Given favorable evidence on the construct validity of teacher evaluation scores as representations of teaching behavior, these scores may be a useful part of the framework for assessing teacher, classroom, and school effects presented by Odden et al. (2004/this issue). In particular, inclusion of evaluation scores in a larger model might make it possible to compare teacher practice effects with effects at other levels and provide evidence for the comparative effectiveness of interventions aimed at affecting teacher practice versus reducing class size or improving principal leadership.

It might be argued that correlations in the .3 to .4 range are relatively small and that they indicate that only a small proportion (9% to 16%) of variance in student achievement was potentially due to variation in teacher performance as measured by this teacher evaluation system. However, it is important to recognize that very high correlations between teacher evaluation scores and student achievement measures are unlikely to be found for reasons including error in measuring teacher performance, error in measuring student performance, lack of alignment between the curriculum taught by teachers and the student tests, and the role of student motivation and related characteristics in producing student learning. It is also likely that the use of EB intercept residuals led to lower correlations than would be found using OLS (or random effects analysis of covariance) residuals because although the former are more reliable, they are also "shrunk" toward zero (Raudenbush & Bryk, 2002, chap. 3), resulting in some restriction of range. This effect was larger for teachers with few students. Also, because the evaluation scores were to be used for administrative purposes, evaluators could have had a tendency to be lenient, therefore restricting the range of variation in evaluation scores and lowering the rating-achievement correlations. Several field studies of performance appraisal scores in other domains (as cited in Murphy & Cleveland, 1995) have found that evaluations done for administrative purposes are more favorable to evaluatees than those done for research purposes.

Limitations and Directions for Future Research

The results presented here should be regarded as suggestive rather than definitive because they are based on only 1 year of student achievement indicators. To address this limitation, we plan to replicate the analyses described here using CPS teacher assessment and student test scores from the 2002–03 school year. Although one would not expect identical correlations in both years, substantial similarity would be expected, providing additional evidence in support of the inference that teachers who score higher on the evaluation system help to produce higher levels of student achievement. Another limitation is the relatively small number of teachers for whom both student test scores and evaluation results are available. This is one potential reason for the considerable variation in correlationship coefficients across subjects and grades. To address this limitation, we plan to use 3 years of teacher evaluation scores to predict student achievement on the 2002–03 round of tests. This will provide a larger sample of teachers and also allow examination of whether the evaluation rating and student achievement relationship weakens as time since the assessment increases. Although one would expect teacher performance to be relatively stable, it is possible that teachers reduce their effort in years they are not evaluated. If this is the case, the relationship of scores to student achievement would weaken. On the other hand, if the assessment encourages skill development or changes in practice, the strength of the relationship should be maintained. The stability of the relationship is important practically because the resource-intensive teacher evaluation process used by CPS cannot realistically be done for every teacher every year. Because student achievement data for 2 years (2001–02 and 2002–03) and 3 years of teacher scores (2000–01, 2001–02, and 2002–03) will be available, it will be possible to make two estimates of the relationship of scores to student achievement 1 year later and one estimate of the relationship between scores and student achievement 2 years later.

Another limitation was that the measure of the achievement of teachers' students used here (the EB intercept residuals from Step 1) was derived from a model that takes the effects of prior year test scores, gender, ethnicity, and poverty as fixed across teachers. A random slopes model may be more realistic in representing the data, but it could increase the potential for overfitting and introduce more complexity into the interpretation. For example, if the slopes of the effect of prior year test scores on current test scores vary, this variation might also be related to teacher evaluation scores. Then deciding who the better teachers are is more complicated than determining who has the higher average student achievement residuals. The degree to which a teacher's students do better or worse than expected will depend on the prior achievement level of the student. A positive relationship between teacher evaluation scores and the slope residual for prior year test scores would not necessarily be desirable because it would imply that more highly rated teachers help students at higher than average levels of prior year achievement more than those at lower than average levels.

References

Binning, J. F., & Barrett, G. V. (1989). Validity of personnel decisions: A conceptual analysis of the inferential and evidential bases. *Journal of Applied Psychology, 74,* 478–494.

Bommer, W. H., Johnson, J. L., Rich, G. A., Podsakoff, P. M., & MacKenzie, S. B. (1995). On the interchangeability of objective and subjective measures or employee performance: A meta-analysis. *Personnel Psychology, 48,* 587–605.

Danielson, C. (1996). *Enhancing professional practice: A framework for teaching.* Alexandria, VA: Association for Supervision and Curriculum Development.

Danielson, C., & McGreal, T. L. (2000). *Teacher evaluation to enhance professional practice.* Alexandria, VA: Association for Supervision and Curriculum Development.

Darling-Hammond, L., Wise, A. E., & Pease, S. R. (1983). Teacher evaluation in the organizational context: A review of the literature. *Review of Educational Research, 53,* 285–328.

Fritsche, L., Weerasinghe, D., & Babu, S. (2003, April). *Making the connection: Linking the teacher evaluation results to the district accountability system.* Paper presented at the American Educational Research Association annual conference, Chicago.

Heneman, R. L. (1986). The relationship between supervisory ratings and results-oriented measures of performance: A meta-analysis. *Personnel Psychology, 39,* 811–826.

Hoaglin, D. C. (1983). Letter values: A set of selected order statistics. In D. C. Hoaglin, F. Mosteller, & J. W. Tukey (Eds.), *Understanding robust and exploratory data analysis* (pp. 33–55). New York: Wiley.

Holtzapple, E. (2002, November). *Validating a teacher evaluation system.* Paper presented at the 2002 annual meeting of the American Evaluation Association, Washington, DC.

Kellor, E., & Odden, A. (2000). *How Cincinnati developed a knowledge and skill-based salary schedule.* Madison, WI: Consortium for Policy Research in Education. Retrieved from http://www.wcer.wisc.edu/cpre/papers/

Medley, D. M., & Coker, H. (1987). The accuracy of principals' judgments of teacher performance. *The Journal of Educational Research, 80,* 242–247.

Messick, S. (1989). Validity. In R. L. Lynn (Ed.), *Educational measurement* (3rd ed., pp. 13–103). Washington, DC: American Council on Education.

Milanowski, A. T., & Heneman, H. G., III. (2001). Assessment of teacher reactions to a standards-based teacher evaluation system: A pilot study. *Journal of Personnel Evaluation in Education, 15,* 193–212.

Murphy, K. R., & Cleveland, J. N. (1995). *Understanding performance appraisal: Social, organizational, and goal-based perspectives.* Thousand Oaks, CA: Sage.

Odden, A., Borman, G., & Fermanich, M. (2004). Assessing teacher, classroom, and school effects, including fiscal effects. *Peabody Journal of Education, 79*(4), 4–32.

Odden, A., & Kelley, C. (2001). *Paying teachers for what they know and do: New and smarter compensation strategies to improve schools* (2nd ed.). Thousand Oaks, CA: Corwin Press.

Peterson, K. D. (2000). *Teacher evaluation: A comprehensive guide to new directions and practices.* Thousand Oaks, CA: Corwin Press.

Porter, A. C., Youngs, P., & Odden, A. (2001). Advances in teacher assessments and their uses. In V. Richardson (Ed.), *Handbook of research on teaching* (4th ed., pp. 259–297). Washington, DC: American Educational Research Association.

Raudenbush, S. W., & Bryk, A. S. (2002). *Hierarchical linear models: Applications and data analysis methods* (2nd ed.). Thousand Oaks, CA: Sage.

Schwab, D. P. (1980). Construct validity in organizational behavior. In B. M. Staw & L. L. Cummings (Eds.), *Research in organizational behavior* (Vol. 2, pp. 3–44). Greenwich, CT: JAI.

Shadish, W. R., & Haddock, C. K. (1994). Combining estimates of effect size. In H. Cooper & L. V. Hedges (Eds.), *The handbook of research synthesis* (pp. 261–281). New York: Russell Sage Foundation.

Stiggens, R. J., & Duke, D. (1988) *The case for commitment to teacher growth: Research on teacher evaluation.* Albany: State University of New York Press.

Appendix

Numbers of Students, Number Tested, and Number Included in Analyses by Grade and Subject

	Third Grade	Fourth Grade	Fifth Grade	Sixth Grade	Seventh Grade	Eighth Grade
Total no. of students on roster in March 2002	3,745	3,358	3,310	3,489	3,289	3,077
No. tested in March 2002						
Reading	3,616	3,235	3,168	3,295	2,788	2,859
Math	3,507	3,228	3,166	3,289	2,793	2,848
Science	0	3,213	3,155	3,202	2,777	2,832
No. for which both 2002 and 2001 test scores are available						
Reading	3,106	2,497	2,574	2,597	2,221	1,943
Math	2,926	2,501	2,593	2,604	2,221	1,951
Science	0	2.393	2,568	2,508	2,201	1,925
Number used in HLM models for step 1 of analyses						
Reading	2,829	2,319	2,395	2,351	1,957	1,819
Math	2,674	2,363	2,455	2,336	1,987	1,823
Science	—	2,238	2,415	2,262	1,923	1,782

Note. HLM = hierarchical linear modeling.

PEABODY JOURNAL OF EDUCATION, 79(4), 54–78

Examining the Relationship Between Teacher Evaluation and Student Assessment Results in Washoe County

Steven M. Kimball, Brad White, and Anthony T. Milanowski
Consortium for Policy Research in Education
University of Wisconsin–Madison

Geoffrey Borman
Department of Educational Administration and Consortium for Policy Research in Education
University of Wisconsin–Madison

In this article, we describe findings from an analysis of the relationship between scores on a standards-based teacher evaluation system modeled on

Previous versions of this article were presented at the March 2003 meeting of the American Educational Finance Association in Orlando, FL and the Annual Meeting of the American Educational Research Association, Chicago, April 2003. We are grateful for the collaboration of Superintendent James Hager, district staff, teachers, and school administrators of the Washoe County School District in this research.

The research reported in this article was supported in part by a grant from the U.S. Department of Education, Office of Educational Research and Improvement, National Institute on Educational Governance, Finance, Policymaking, and Management to the Consortium for Policy Research in Education (CPRE) and the Wisconsin Center for Education Research, School of Education, University of Wisconsin–Madison (Grant OERI–R3086A60003). The opinions expressed are those of the authors and do not necessarily reflect the view of the National Institute on Educational Governance, Finance, Policymaking, and Management, Office of Educational Research and Improvement, U.S. Department of Education; the institutional partners of CPRE; or the Wisconsin Center for Education Research.

Requests for reprints should be sent to Steven M. Kimball, University of Wisconsin–Madison, Consortium for Policy Research in Education, 1025 West Johnson Street, Madison, WI 53706. E-mail: skimball@education.wisc.edu the Framework for Teaching (Danielson, 1996) and student achievement measures in a large Western school district. We apply multilevel statistical modeling to study the relationship between the evaluation scores and state and district tests of reading, mathematics, and a composite measure of reading and mathematics. Using a value-added framework, the teacher evaluation scores were included at the 2nd level, or teacher level, of the model when other student and teacher-level characteristics were controlled. This study provided some initial evidence of a positive association between teacher performance, as measured by the evaluation system, and student achievement. The coefficients representing the effects of teacher performance on student achievement were positive and were statistically significant in 4 of 9 grade–test combinations studied.

The quest for valid and consistent measures of teacher behaviors that are related to student learning has long been pursued in educational research and school improvement endeavors. The identification of such measures could help inform a variety of important educational purposes including instructional improvement and accountability, professional development, finance and personnel resource allocations, and teacher compensation reform (Odden, Borman, & Fermanich, 2004/this issue). In the search for adequate measures of teacher or classroom effects on student achievement, teacher performance assessment results could be considered as one possible alternative if the evaluation scores can be shown to be valid measures of teaching practice and to have the expected positive relationship to student achievement.

New, standards-based teacher evaluation practices have recently emerged to respond to historical deficiencies in evaluation practices and improve instruction and accountability (Danielson & McGreal, 2000; Davis, Pool, & Mits-Cash, 2000; Kimball, 2002; Milanowski & Heneman, 2001). As discussed by Milanowski (2004/this issue), not only do these evaluation reforms provide a promising new direction in school personnel evaluation practices, but also the results from evaluations may represent a useful source of information on classroom or teacher effects on student achievement.

The standards-based teacher evaluation system implemented in Nevada's Washoe County School District (WCSD) provides an interesting contrast to the system in Cincinnati Public Schools (Milanowski, 2004/this issue). Although both districts based their evaluation systems on the standards and evidence sources recommended in the Framework for Teaching (Danielson, 1996), Washoe County represents a more typical adaptation of the standards and a more common type of teacher evaluation process. Unlike Cincinnati, Washoe made few changes to the evaluation standards and did not design its evaluation system for use in high-stakes decisions such as salary determinations. Instead, the evaluation system was designed for low-stakes purposes. It was intended to provide a comprehensive and research-based conception of teaching quality that would guide evaluation discussions, promote formative feedback and teacher reflection on instruction, and substantiate summative evaluation judgments including contract renewal and tenure decisions.

If the teaching standards included in the Framework-based evaluation systems, such as those implemented in Washoe County, represent quality teaching, then one might expect that assessments of teaching behaviors using the standards will reflect measures of student achievement (Milanowski, 2004/this issue). In this article, we explore this hypothesis by analyzing the relationship between teacher behavior, as measured through the evaluation system, and the amount of student achievement attributable to teachers. A positive relationship would provide evidence for the criterion-related validity of the evaluation system and provide a reason to pursue the use of evaluation scores as measures of teacher practice in broader research contexts. Following a brief review of system implementation in Washoe County, the analysis turns to the key question underlying standards-based teacher evaluation reform innovations: Do teachers who score well on such evaluation systems also help produce higher levels of student learning?

Implementation Context

The WCSD encompasses the cities of Reno and Sparks, Nevada, and their outlying areas. The district is the second largest in the state, with over 58,000 students and 84 schools. Thirty-eight percent of the students are non-White, and two thirds of the minority student population is Hispanic. There are over 3,700 certified staff and about 270 administrators working in the district (Washoe County School District, 2003).

In 1997, the WCSD and Washoe County Teachers' Association came to an agreement that teacher evaluation practices in the district were deficient and that they needed a system that would facilitate teacher growth and strengthen instructional accountability. District and association officials recommended a new system that would empower teachers and allow them input into the evaluation process, reduce top-down communication, and attempt to standardize evaluation quality across evaluators (Sawyer, 2001). In addition, the officials wanted a system that would differentiate teacher performance using rubrics that delineated weak to strong instructional behaviors. Under the prior system, examples of exemplary performance were described, but the evaluations resulted only in ratings of satisfactory or unsatisfactory. Because the system lacked multiple performance rubrics, both marginally performing and strongly performing teachers could receive the same satisfactory ratings. The district desired a system based on a progressive set of teaching expectations to monitor and guide a teacher's performance.

A task force made up of members of the teachers' association, principals' association, district staff, and the school board worked collaboratively to restructure the system for evaluating teachers. The task force researched a number of evaluation design alternatives and chose the standards and procedures included in the Framework for Teaching (Danielson, 1996). This evaluation system is intended to measure four domains of practice: planning and preparation (Domain 1), classroom environment (Domain 2), instruction (Domain 3), and professional responsibilities (Domain 4). Each domain has a number of teaching "components," and every component has several "elements." As adapted by the district, each element includes separate behavioral descriptions on a four-level rubric: unsatisfactory, target for growth (Level 1), proficient (Level 2), and area of strength (Level 3). There are 23 components of professional practice and 68 elements in the Washoe County system. The following is an example of one element (knowledge of prerequisite relationships) from the Demonstrating Knowledge of Content and Pedagogy component of the Planning and Preparation domain:

- *Unsatisfactory:* Teacher displays little understanding of prerequisite knowledge important for student learning of the content.
- *Target for growth* (Level 1): Teacher indicates some awareness of prerequisite learning, although such knowledge may be incomplete or inaccurate.
- *Proficient* (Level 2): Teacher's plans and practices reflect understanding of prerequisite relationships among topics and concepts.
- *Area of strength* (Level 3): Teacher actively builds on knowledge of prerequisite relationships when describing instruction or seeking causes for student misunderstanding.

The new, standards-based evaluation system was launched in 2000 after 1 year of planning and 2 years of field testing. The evaluation system calls for multiple sources of evidence to demonstrate teacher performance relative to the standards. Principals or assistant principals serve as teacher evaluators, and they have some discretion in the specific sources of evidence to gather and how the evidence is applied to the standards to make evaluation decisions. Evidence may include a teacher self-assessment, a preobservation data sheet (lesson plan), classroom and nonclassroom observations with preobservation and postobservation conferences, instructional artifacts (e.g., assignments and student work), a reflection form, a 3-week unit plan, and logs of professional activities and parent contacts. Departing from recommendations by Danielson (1996), there is no instructional portfolio requirement. The combined sources of evidence are intended to provide the basis for evaluators' formative and summative evaluation decisions and related performance feedback.

In the system, teachers advance through three evaluation stages: probationary, postprobationary major, and postprobationary minor. All teachers undergo one of these three stages each year. Teachers who are novice teachers or new to the district are considered probationary and are evaluated on all four of the performance domains in which they must meet at least Level 1 (target for growth) scores on all 68 elements. Probationary teachers are observed at least nine times over three periods of the year, and a written evaluation is provided at the end of each period; based on their performance, they may be required to undergo a second probationary year, be advanced to postprobationary status, or be dismissed from teaching in the district.

Teachers in postprobationary status undergo a "major evaluation" on two performance domains. They are formally observed three times over the course of the year and receive one written evaluation at the end of the year. Once teachers are successfully evaluated under the major evaluation, they move to two "minor evaluation" years. Teachers on the postprobationary minor cycle are evaluated on one domain and are formally observed at least once during the year. Each year of the 2-year minor evaluation results in one written, year-end evaluation. As a result of the evaluation cycle, most teachers are not evaluated on the same domains each year but instead will have all four domains evaluated over a 3-year cycle. For each evaluation, any standard rated unsatisfactory results in an overall unsatisfactory score and the teacher participates in a structured intervention process that results in the teacher moving back into the regular major–minor cycle or the initiation of dismissal proceedings.

Method

Prior research on the impact of the teacher evaluation system in Washoe County has suggested that teachers and administrators agree with and accept the new performance standards and evaluation process (Kimball, 2001). Here, we expand the research scope to explore the relationship between evaluation scores and student achievement. To the extent that the teacher evaluation scores have a positive relationship with student achievement measures, there will be some evidence that the evaluation system can identify teachers who, by one measure of teaching effectiveness, are producing better results. The analysis will provide evidence of the ability of the evaluation system to distinguish between teachers whose classes show different levels of average student achievement. A substantial positive relationship between evaluation scores and student achievement would suggest that helping teachers improve their practice in accordance with the teaching standards has the potential to contribute to improvements in student learning.

Given the multiple levels of data in this analysis, with students nested in classrooms, we applied multilevel statistical modeling (Raudenbush & Bryk, 2002; Snijders & Bosker, 1999) to estimate the random effects of classrooms on mathematics and reading achievement across three grades. Using hierarchical linear modeling (HLM) software (Raudenbush, Bryk, Cheong, & Congdon, 2001), several two-level models were estimated. The basic strategy at Level 1 was to predict students' posttest scores in reading and mathematics from their demographics and pretest scores. At Level 2, predictors included the teacher's evaluation score and other potentially relevant teacher characteristics. In this way, we estimated the effect of attending a classroom taught by a teacher with a higher or lower evaluation score after statistically controlling student background and other conventional measures of teacher quality.

Measures

Student achievement. We collected several measures of student achievement, including 2000–01 and 2001–02 results from district, state, and national norm-referenced tests for third-, fourth-, and fifth-grade students in mathematics and reading. The tests used for each grade level analysis are presented in Table 1.

Table 1

Student Achievement Measures by Grade

Grade	Pretest	Posttest
3	District CRT (spring 2001)	State CRT (spring 2002)
4	Terra Nova (fall 2001)	Terra Nova (spring 2002)
5	Terra Nova (spring 2001)	State CRT (spring 2002)

Note. CRT = criterion-referenced test.

The pretest for the third-grade students was a second-grade district criterion-referenced test (CRT) from spring 2001, and the posttest was a spring 2002 state-administered CRT. The fourth-grade student pretest was the Comprehensive Test of Basic Skills (5th edition; CTBS/5), Terra Nova norm-referenced test administered in October 2001, and the posttest was the Terra Nova exam administered in April 2002. The pretest for fifth-grade students was the Terra Nova administered in spring 2001, when these students were in fourth grade. The posttest for these students was the fifth-grade state CRT administered in spring 2002.

Each test was aligned to the state academic content standards. At the elementary level, the district administers criterion-referenced exams it has developed for 1st, 2nd, 4th, and 6th grades.[1] The state administers criterion-referenced exams developed by Harcourt Brace for 3rd- and 5th-grade students. Test items include both constructed and written responses. Individual scaled-score results on the 5th-grade state CRT were used for the 5th-grade analysis. The Terra Nova exams was used as part of the Nevada Proficiency Examination Program that requires norm-referenced testing to be administered in Grades 4, 8, and 10 in reading, language, mathematics, and science (La Marca, 1999). Students were assessed on selected-response items, and results were reported in composite and scaled scores. Scaled-score results were used for our analysis. The Terra Nova was administered statewide in October, and the district also administered the Terra Nova in the spring to 4th-grade students to allow for an assessment of achievement growth over 1 academic year. The Terra Nova has since been discontinued and replaced with the Iowa Test of Basic Skills.

A substantial proportion of the students enrolled in each grade in the 2001–02 school year could not be included in the analysis because either or both the pretest and posttest scores were not available. Other students could not be included because their teachers were not evaluated on the evaluation standards used for this analysis during the 2001–02 school year, because other data were missing, or because they could not be matched with a single classroom teacher. As a result of these factors, 43% of the students tested in third grade were available for the analysis. About 45% of the tested fourth- and fifth-grade students were included in the analysis. Appendix A shows the total number of students by grade, the numbers for whom test scores were available, and the number of students included in the final sample.

---

[1]Due to incomplete data or large amounts of missing records, results from the first- and sixth-grade exams could not be utilized in this study, and the value-added analysis was not conducted for students in second and sixth grade. If available, these exam results will be used in future analyses.

Other student (Level 1) variables.   The district also provided data on other student characteristics including ethnicity, gender, free/reduced-price lunch status, and special education status. This information was used to construct a set of dummy variables for gender (female = 1), minority status (non-White = 1), free/reduced-price lunch (recipient of free/reduced-price lunch = 1), and special education status (recipient of special education services = 1). These variables, along with the pretest scores, were included as controls at Level 1 of the HLM described next. Appendix B provides descriptive statistics from the sample of students and teachers used in the analyses.

Teacher performance.   Teacher evaluation scores from the 2001 to 2002 school year were obtained for each teacher who could be matched to students with pretest and posttest scores. As previously mentioned, the evaluation system design results in some teachers being evaluated on one or more teaching domains depending on their status in the evaluation cycle. If a teacher is not evaluated on the instruction domain, they are evaluated using a supplemental evaluation form (which we refer to as the *performance composite*). The supplemental evaluation form consists of selected components and elements from Domain 1 (planning and preparation) and Domain 3 (instruction), representing 7 out of 23 evaluation components. As with the rubrics for the 68 elements, the composite standards were evaluated using four performance designations (i.e., unsatisfactory, target for growth, proficient, and area of strength). The composite standards follow:

- The teaching displays solid content knowledge and uses a repertoire of current pedagogical practices for the discipline being taught (reference: Components 1a, 1c, 3e).
- The teaching is designed coherently using a logical sequence, matching materials and resources appropriately, and using a well-defined structure for connecting the individual activities to the entire unit. Instruction links student assessment data to instructional planning and implementation (reference: Components 1f, 1e, 3f).
- The teaching provides for adjustments in planned lessons to match the students' needs more specifically. The teacher is persistent in using alternative approaches and strategies for students who are not initially successful (reference: Component 3e).
- The teaching engages students cognitively in activities and assignments, groups are productive, and strategies are congruent to instructional objectives (reference: Component 3c).

We chose to focus the analysis of teacher evaluation scores on the performance composite measure because although there are a limited number of standards included in the performance composite, the measure represents key elements from two domains relating to instructional practice. In addition, more teachers received evaluation scores for the performance composite than for any one domain. Probationary teachers are evaluated on all domains, and they do not receive the composite scores; however, we were able to compute a composite score by combining the same elements that make up the performance composite, allowing us to include probationary teachers in the study. Similarly, we were able to include those teachers on the major cycle who were evaluated on Domains 1 and 3 but did not have an evaluation on the composite evaluation form because the instruction domain was covered.

The scores on the four performance composites were averaged to derive a single indicator for teacher quality as defined by the evaluation system. As shown in Appendix C, the intercorrlations between the performance composites ranged from .56 to .86 across the three grades. Cronbach's coefficient alpha for our indicator of teacher quality derived from the four composites was .87 for Grade 3, .89 for Grade 4, and .91 for Grade 5, indicating high internal consistency for the measure.

Unfortunately, there were still some teachers with evaluation scores that could not be included in the analysis because they were evaluated on different domains and elements and therefore did not have comparable scores. About 50% to 70% of the teachers for which we had matches to student achievement data and evaluation scores were included at each grade. Included in the final analysis were 123 third-grade teachers, 87 fourth-grade teachers, and 118 fifth-grade teachers.

Other teacher (Level 2) variables. In addition to the teacher evaluation scores, in some of the analyses, we included a combined measure of teachers' education and experience derived from the district salary schedule. Rather than including separate measures of experience and education/training, this combined variable was used in part due to the correlation between our measures of experience and education. Further, using this combined measure allowed for an exploration of whether a relationship existed between teachers' placement on the salary schedule and student achievement.

Finally, because there were 15 elementary schools that operated on a year-round calendar at the time of the study, we controlled for potential differences in results for students attending schools with these different academic schedules. This was particularly important in Grade 4 because there were differences across schools in the number of instructional days between the fall and spring administrations of the Terra Nova. Arguably, this variable would be more appropriately included as a third- (school-) level variable. Unfortunately, we did not have enough schools and teachers within schools to estimate a meaningful three-level model. Therefore, a dummy variable (year-round = 1) was included at the teacher level to represent whether a teacher's class was on the traditional or year-round schedule.

Analysis

As a first step in the analysis, an unconditional, or "empty," model was used to get an estimate of the total variance in test scores at the student and teacher levels. Then, a random intercept model was estimated with explanatory variables (pretest and student demographics) at Level 1 and no Level 2 predictors. This showed how much Level 2 variance was available to be explained by teacher evaluation scores and other teacher characteristics after controlling for the Level 1 predictors. Next, the Level 2, or teacher-level, prediction models were estimated for the random intercepts. These represented the primary analyses used to address the question of the relationship between evaluation scores and classroom mean achievement. A random slope model was then estimated in which the slopes of the relationship of pretest to posttest were allowed to vary by teacher. Finally, teacher evaluation scores were included as Level 2 predictors of the random slopes of the pretest–posttest relationship.

For the primary analysis, the model at Level 1 was

$$\text{Posttest} = \beta_0 + \beta_1\text{Pretest} + \beta_2\text{Female} + \beta_3\text{Non-White} + \beta_4\text{Special Education} + \beta_5\text{FRL} + R,$$

which represents achievement on the posttest regressed on the pretest score, gender, minority status, special education status, free- and reduced-lunch status, and the Level 1 residual variance (R). All Level 1 predictors were grand-mean centered. The Level 2 model was

$$\beta_0 = \gamma_{00} + \gamma_{01}\text{Evaluation Score} + \gamma_{02}\text{Education/Experience} + \gamma_{03}\text{Year-Round Schedule} + U_0$$
$$\beta_1 = \gamma_{10}$$
$$\beta_2 = \gamma_{20}$$
$$\beta_3 = \gamma_{30}$$
$$\beta_4 = \gamma_{40}$$
$$\beta_5 = \gamma_{50},$$

where the classroom mean achievement is regressed on the teacher evaluation score, education and experience of the teacher, whether the classroom is on a year-round schedule, and the classroom residual variance (U_0). Level 2 predictors were not grand-mean centered, and the slopes for all (β_1–β_5) Level 1 variables were treated as fixed for this analysis.

Because most students were instructed in both mathematics and reading by the same teacher and tested in both subjects in spring 2002, these scores were averaged to create a composite test score for each student. These composite scores were also used to study the relationship between student achievement and the teacher evaluation scores. Separate analyses of mathematics and reading achievement were also conducted. The evaluation system is not subject-matter specific; therefore, combining the two exams allowed an exploration of whether the system was picking up more general pedagogical skill that would be reflected in achievement on the combined tests.

Results

Table 2 reports the proportion of current year test score variance at the teacher level and the reliabilities of the random intercepts at the teacher level for the model with controls for prior year achievement and other student characteristics at Level 1. The table shows that approximately 17% to 27% of the variance in student achievement for each assessment at each grade was at the teacher level without controlling for prior test scores and student characteristics and between 5% to 15% after controlling for these

Table 2

Percentage of Test Score Variance at Teacher Level From Empty Model Compared With Level 1 Covariates and Reliability of Random Intercepts

| Grade | Test | % Variance at Level 2 | | Reliability of Random Intercepts From Model With Level 1 Covariates |
		Empty Model	Model With Level 1 Covariates	
3	Reading	16.87	5.44	.513
3	Math	18.84	9.64	.656
3	Combined	20.71	8.49	.625
4	Reading	21.35	7.90	.644
4	Math	23.74	14.70	.799
4	Combined	26.48	13.67	.765
5	Reading	21.25	7.89	.648
5	Math	23.73	13.10	.759
5	Combined	26.67	12.17	.744

factors. These results suggest that there is sufficient reliable variation in student achievement at the teacher level to be related to teacher evaluation scores. The chi-square tests for random effects of U_0 were significant for each test in each grade, indicating that average achievement does differ between teachers' classes after controlling for the Level 1 variables.

Teacher Evaluation Effect

The next analysis was aimed at estimating the relationship between the teacher evaluation scores from the performance composite and student achievement while controlling for prior student achievement and the other student characteristics at Level 1 and only the teacher evaluation composite score included at Level 2. This represents the simplest assessment of criterion-related validity because it estimates the relationship between evaluation scores and student achievement without any other potential teacher characteristics or other influences being controlled at the teacher level.[2] Table 3 presents the results from the random intercept model including the student pretest scores and other characteristics controlled at Level 1 and only the teacher evaluation scores at Level 2.

As shown in Table 3, the results are mixed as to whether the teacher evaluation score is a statistically significant predictor of student achievement after controlling for prior achievement and various student characteristics. The evaluation score was a statistically significant and positive predictor of student achievement in four of the nine models, each at or less than the .01 alpha level. These results suggest that for every 1-point increase in teacher evaluation scores, student performance on the fourth-grade reading assessment increased 5.41 points. The teacher evaluation score was not a significant predictor of math achievement or the combined results at the fourth grade. With a 1-point increase in fifth-grade teacher's evaluation score, student performance increased 12.66 points in reading, 20.08 in math, and 16.29 points on the math and reading combination. Although the coefficients were positive for the third-grade results, they were not statistically significant.

Correlation of Bayes residuals and evaluation scores. Another way to examine the criterion-related validity of the evaluation system is by correlating the empirical Bayes intercept residuals, which represents the average student performance attributed to each teacher, with the teacher evaluation scores. We calculated the Bayes residuals with all Level 1 variables in-

---

[2]There was little difference in the results for the teacher evaluation coefficients when the analyses were run with only the student pretest scores controlled at Level 1.

Table 3

Teacher-Level Results of Random Intercept Model Including Teacher Evaluation Scores

Teacher-Level Variable	Third Grade			Fourth Grade			Fifth Grade		
	Coefficient	*SE*	*p*	*Coefficient*	*SE*	*p*	*Coefficient*	*SE*	*p*
Reading evaluation score	5.10	4.78	.287	5.41	2.09	.010	12.66	3.91	.002
Math evaluation score	6.71	5.88	.254	1.20	2.32	.603	20.08	4.48	.000
Combined math and reading evaluation score	5.28	4.98	.289	3.18	1.99	.111	16.29	3.86	.000

cluded and with only the pretest scores included at Level 1. Excluding the other variables at Level 1 might result in more variance available at Level 2 that could be related to performance on the teacher evaluation system. The correlations of the residuals with the evaluation scores including the Level 1 variables were .101 for third-grade reading and math, .279 for fourth-grade reading, .068 for fourth-grade math, .281 for fifth-grade reading, and .374 for fifth-grade math. Consistent with the coefficients from the HLM analysis, there were statistically significant results for the fourth-grade reading and both fifth-grade tests but not for the third-grade results. Dropping the other Level 1 variables did not substantially change the results.

Other Level 2 Variables

In the next analysis, we added variables for the combination of education and experience and a dummy variable indicating which classrooms were on year-round schedules. Table 4 shows the results at Level 2. The coefficients for the student-level variables are also displayed in Appendix D for interested readers.

Education/experience.   Like the teacher evaluation scores, teacher education and experience also did not consistently display a statistically significant relationship to student achievement. There were positive but weak effects on student achievement in the fifth-grade math, reading, and the combined test, but the results on the third- and fourth-grade tests were not statistically significant. The results at the fifth grade suggest that a 1-unit increase in the education and experience measure (equivalent to $1,000 on the salary schedule) was related to approximately a ½-point increase on each of the two exams and combined measure. These results are similar to findings in the teacher quality literature that suggest mixed or weak effects of teacher experience and education on student achievement (Wayne & Youngs, 2003).

Year-round effect.   The final variable included was whether or not students were taught in classes that operated on a year-round or traditional school calendar. Interestingly, the year-round school variable was a statistically significant and negative predictor in all but three of the grade–subject combinations. In fourth grade, this result may have been due to students in year-round schools having potentially longer vacation breaks between the pretests and posttests than students in schools following the traditional calendar. However, this explanation does not apply to Grades 3 and 5, so further investigation would be necessary to account for this finding.

Table 4

Teacher-Level Results From Final Random Intercept Model

Teacher-Level Variables	Third Grade			Fourth Grade			Fifth Grade		
	Coefficient	*SE*	*p*	*Coefficient*	*SE*	*p*	*Coefficient*	*SE*	*p*
Reading model									
Evaluation score	4.74	5.51	.390	5.61	2.00	.005	10.35	3.93	.009
Education and experience	0.04	0.24	.858	0.05	0.11	.673	0.44	0.17	.010
Year-round schedule	-4.50	3.78	.235	-5.64	1.90	.003	-5.75	3.90	.140
Math model									
Evaluation score	5.41	6.48	.404	1.73	2.14	.419	17.25	4.47	.000
Education and experience	0.17	0.31	.580	-0.05	0.13	.706	0.48	0.19	.015
Year-round schedule	-11.32	4.72	.017	-7.49	2.02	.000	-12.88	4.39	.004
Combined reading and math model									
Evaluation score	4.51	5.6	.421	3.51	1.85	.058	13.70	3.81	.001
Education and experience	0.10	0.25	.685	0.03	0.11	.800	0.46	0.16	.004
Year-round schedule	-6.67	3.90	.087	-6.86	1.71	.000	-9.65	3.81	.012

Slope Variation

The next analysis modified the model to allow the slope of the Level 1 relationship of pretest to posttest to vary among teachers. Although very small in absolute terms, each of the fourth-grade results and two of the third-grade results (reading and the combined test results) showed statistically significant variance in these slopes. None of the fifth-grade results showed statistically significant slope variance. The result in fourth grade could be due to relative consistency among the fourth-grade classes because students generally had the same teacher for pretest and posttest and because the exams were similar (both were different forms of the Terra Nova). The explanation would not apply to the third-grade results in which the pretests and posttests occurred in different school years. Adding the teacher evaluation measure to predict these random slopes was not statistically significant in the third-grade tests but did lead to statistically significant results for the fourth-grade math and combined tests. For the fourth-grade math test, the Level 2 random intercept coefficient for the teacher evaluation scores increased by about 0.66 (from 1.73 to 2.39). For the other exams, the coefficients for the teacher evaluation scores remained essentially the same.

Evaluation Score Versus Education/Experience

Finally, to get some idea of the relative strength of the teacher evaluation score in comparison with education and experience as predictors of student achievement, to determine the reduction in variance at Level 2 (teacher level), each predictor was added separately to the random intercept model with Level 1 controls. As shown in Table 5, for six of the nine

Table 5

Percentage of Level 2 Variance Explained by Evaluation Score Versus Education and Experience Combination

Grade	Test	Variance Component at Level 2, Model With Covariates at Level 1	% Reduction in Variance Component From Adding Evaluation Score	% Reduction in Variance Component From Adding Education and Experience
3	Reading	186.59	0	0
3	Math	425.10	0.27	0
3	Combined	261.29	0	0
4	Reading	45.74	8.4	0
4	Math	82.79	0	0
4	Combined	57.14	1.4	0
5	Reading	228.33	10.34	7.9
5	Math	408.66	16.6	8.2
5	Combined	272.28	16.5	9.9

grade/tests, the teacher evaluation scores explained more Level 2 (be-tween-teacher variance) than the experience and education composite measure. The proportion of Level 2 variance explained by the evaluation scores ranged from 0% to 16.6%, whereas the proportion explained by education and experience ranged from 0% to 9.9%.

Discussion and Conclusions

The results of our study were mixed with respect to the question of whether teachers' scores on the Washoe County teacher evaluation system were related to the average achievement of those teachers' students, pro-viding only tentative evidence for the criterion-related validity of the eval-uation system and use of evaluation scores as measures of classroom effects for other research or educational intervention purposes. The es-timated relationship of the teacher evaluation scores to student achieve-ment was positive for each grade and subject and for the reading and math composite, but the coefficients were not statistically significant in all cases. For fourth-grade reading and for each test at Grade 5, the coefficient for the evaluation score was positive and statistically significant. For the other grades and exams, the corresponding coefficients were not significant. However, compared to education and experience as reflected in the district salary schedule, the teacher evaluation scores do help explain more varia-tion in teacher effects.

There are several possible reasons why stronger effects were not found. In addition to the potential for measurement error and other confounding factors (e.g., potential lack of alignment between what is taught and stu-dent exams) that may be found in most value-added studies (see Milanow-ski, 2004/this issue), the evaluation performance composite used in this study represented only 7 of the 23 evaluation components from the teacher evaluation system. Therefore, we could be missing some important infor-mation about teacher performance. The limited representation of perfor-mance scores may have restricted the range of variation among teachers compared to a more comprehensive performance measure.

The utility of the district exams for value-added analysis was also lim-ited. Results of the second-grade district CRT, which was used as the pre-test for the third-grade analysis, had a non-normal distribution. With mean test scores of 79 (out of 100) for second-grade reading and 89 for math, there was clearly a restricted range of test scores that could be related to achievement in the third grade. Transformations of the pretest results did not improve the overall results.

Another reason for the mixed results could be related to the context of teacher evaluation in the district. Although evaluation decisions could lead to nonrenewal or formal dismissal proceedings, such actions are rare. Given the relatively low stakes nature of the evaluation system, it is possible that evaluators were less focused on differentiating teacher performance than they were on improving staff morale through positive feedback and helping teachers identify areas of growth. The result could be lower reliability of evaluation ratings. Indeed, prior research has suggested that in addition to evaluator emphasis on teacher praise and growth, the evidence gathered tends to vary between evaluators (Kimball, 2001). In addition, there has not been a heavy emphasis on evaluation training and oversight for consistency and accuracy. In contrast, the systems in Cincinnati (Milanowski, 2004/this issue) and Vaughn Elementary School (Gallagher, 2004/this issue) were designed for higher stakes, contained multiple raters, and employed more extensive training for rater consistency.

It is also possible that the standards are not specific enough to comprehensively assess teacher performance on key aspects of instruction. It would be interesting to study whether results would have been different if the evaluation system focused more on instructional content and content-specific pedagogy and emphasized uniform sources of teaching evidence. This evaluation system, like others structured closely on the Framework for Teaching (Danielson, 1996), is generic with respect to instructional content. That is, the same evaluation instrument is used for teachers regardless of the content they teach or the grade level of their students. In contrast to the system studied by Gallagher (2004/this issue), the Washoe County system used no content-specific evaluation standards. Although the standards in the Washoe system encourage evaluators to look at the specific content teachers teach and how they teach it, the interpretation is largely up to the individual evaluator. It is possible that tailoring the system to include more content-specific elements may better capture important aspects of instruction. In addition, applying more uniform sources of teaching evidence, such as the structured instructional portfolio approach and use of classroom videotapes recommended by Odden (2003), may provide better and more consistent evidence of instructional content and content-specific pedagogy. With these changes, we would expect improved measures of validity associated with the evaluation system.

Finally, an interesting result was the lower level of average achievement of students in classes that operated with a year-round academic calendar. Although a detailed exploration of these results was beyond the scope of this study, results of a meta-analysis on the effects of modified school calendars on student achievement conducted by Cooper, Valentine, Charlton, and Melson (2003) suggest that although mixed on average, students from low socioeconomic backgrounds attending schools on modified schedules performed better than their peers in traditional schedule classrooms. An initial examination of our results was inconclusive on average achievement differences for students from low economic backgrounds in the year-round schools. A more comprehensive investigation of these findings would be worth pursuing in future studies.

Limitations and Future Research

This study has several limitations that we will seek to address in future analyses. First, the results are based on only 1 year's worth of data, which yielded tentative conclusions about the value added from a teacher's individual performance. Second, as mentioned previously, the study applied a composite performance measure that may not have captured the full scope of variation in teacher performance as assessed in the evaluation system. Third, a substantial number of students were lost from the analysis due to missing assessment data.

To address these limitations, we intend to collect teacher evaluation and student achievement data for 2 more years. This extension will allow for the replication of results and should provide a broader base for conclusions about the criterion-related validity of the Washoe system. In addition, we will be working with the district to better track test data and maximize the number of teachers and students in the analyses. We also intend to do more analyses with the subset of teachers for whom scores on more of the performance elements used in the evaluation system are available. This will provide some evidence as to whether the performance composites we used were adequate in representing the aspects of teacher performance that are related to student achievement.

The study did not thoroughly examine slope differences due to considerations of time, space, and a desire to retain a parsimonious model. It might be useful in further studies to explore what may be contributing to different slopes in the third- and fourth-grade data and whether slope differences exist in other grades. Different specifications of the models at Level 1 will be compared to those applied in this study to address slope differences and the presence of floor and ceiling effects.

A study is currently being conducted to determine if the evaluation scores given by some evaluators are more strongly associated with average student achievement than those given by others. A preliminary investigation suggests that such variation does exist. If some evaluators' scores are more strongly associated with student achievement, these evaluators may be, in one sense, better judges of teacher performance. By studying these evaluators, it might be possible to find out whether they used different evidence, had better skills, or used a different decision-making process than those whose evaluation scores were not as strongly related to student achievement. If systematic differences between evaluators emerge, this may become the basis for efforts to improve evaluator training in standards-based teacher evaluation systems as well as providing insight into evaluator decision processes.

References

Cooper, H., Valentine, J. C., Charlton, K., & Melson, A. (2003). The effects of modified school calendars on student achievement and on school and community attitudes. *Review of Educational Research, 73*, 1–52.

Danielson, C. (1996). *Enhancing professional practice: A framework for teaching.* Alexandria, VA: Association for Supervision and Curriculum Development.

Danielson, C., & McGreal, T. L. (2000). *Teacher evaluation to enhance professional practice.* Alexandria, VA: Association for Supervision and Curriculum Development.

Davis, D. R., Pool, J. E., & Mits-Cash, M. (2000). Issues in implementing a new teacher assessment system in a large urban school district: Results of a qualitative field study. *Journal of Personnel Evaluation in Education, 14,* 285–306.

Gallagher, H. A. (2004/this issue). Vaughn Elementary's innovative teacher evaluation system: Are teacher evaluation scores related to growth in student achievement? *Peabody Journal of Education, 79*(4), 79–107.

Kimball, S. M. (2001). *Innovations in teacher evaluation: Case studies of two school districts with teacher evaluation systems based on the framework for teaching.* Ann Arbor, MI: UMI Dissertations Publishing.

Kimball, S. M. (2002). Analysis of feedback, enabling conditions and fairness perceptions of teachers in three school districts with new standards-based evaluation systems. *Journal of Personnel Evaluation in Education, 16,* 241–268.

La Marca, P. M. (1999). *Results of statewide TerraNova testing, fall 1998* (Prepared for Nevada Proficiency Examination program). Carson City, NV: Nevada Department of Education.

Milanowski, A. (2004/this issue). The relationship between teacher performance evaluation scores and student achievement: Evidence from Cincinnati. *Peabody Journal of Education, 79*(4), 33–53.

Milanowski, A. T., & Heneman, H. G., III. (2001). Assessment of teacher reactions to a standards-based teacher evaluation system: A pilot study. *Journal of Personnel Evaluation in Education, 15,* 193–212.

Odden, A. R. (2003). An early assessment of comprehensive teacher compensation change plans. In M. L. Plecki & D. H. Monk (Vol. Eds.), *Yearbook of the American Education Finance Association 2003: School finance and teacher quality: Exploring the connections* (pp. 209–228). Larchmont, NY: Eye on Education.

Odden, A., Borman, G., & Fermanich, M. (2004/this issue). Assessing teacher, classroom, and school effects, including fiscal effects. *Peabody Journal of Education, 79*(4), 4–32.

Raudenbush, S. W., & Bryk, A. S. (2002). *Hierarchical linear models: Applications and data analysis methods* (2nd ed.). Thousand Oaks, CA: Sage.

Raudenbush, S., Bryk, S., Cheong, U. F., & Congdon, R. (2001). *HLM 5: Hierarchical linear and nonlinear modeling.* Lincolnwood, IL: Scientific Software International, Inc.

Sawyer, L. (2001). Revamping a teacher evaluation system. *Educational Leadership, 58*(5), 44–47.

Snijders, T., & Bosker, R. J. (1999). *Multilevel analysis: An introduction to basic and advanced multilevel modeling*. Thousand Oaks, CA: Sage.

Wayne, A. J., & Youngs, P. (2003). Teacher characteristics and student achievement gains: A review. *Review of Educational Research, 73*, 89–122.

Washoe County School District. (2003). *Fast facts*. Retrieved June 10, 2003, from www.washoe.k12.nv.us/district/facts

Appendix A

Number of Students, Number Tested, and Number Included in Analysis by Grade and Subject

Student Group	Third Grade	Fourth Grade	Fifth Grade
On active roster	4,731	4,867	4,885
Tested in spring 2002			
Reading	4,317	3,965	4,571
Math	4,382	3,985	4,595
Both pre- and posttest scores available			
Reading	2,637	3,800	3,678
Math	2,698	3,838	3,697
In HLM models			
Reading	1,871	1,783	2,122
Math	1,882	1,803	2,131
Combined reading and math	1,858	1,752	2,073

Note. HLM = hierarchical linear modeling.

Appendix B

Descriptive Statistics

Variable	N	M	SD	Minimum	Maximum
Grade 3					
Teacher level					
Evaluation score	123	2.67	0.39	1.55	3.00
Education and experience	123	43,488.87	7,858.63	29,331.00	54,799.00
Year-round schedule	123	0.33	0.47	0.00	1.00
Student level					
Reading pretest score	1,871	79.37	16.93	17.50	100.00
Reading posttest score	2,216	298.04	74.33	100.00	500.00
Math pretest score	1,882	88.95	11.06	22.50	100.00
Math posttest score	2,239	293.52	80.07	100.00	500.00
Composite pretest score	1,858	84.27	12.93	27.50	100.00
Composite posttest score	2,194	296.94	71.32	100.00	500.00
Female	2,261	.49	0.50	0.00	1.00
Non-White	2,398	0.38	0.48	0.00	1.00
Special education	2,398	0.13	0.34	0.00	1.00
Free/Reduced-price lunch	2,398	0.35	0.48	0.00	1.00
Grade 4					
Teacher level					
Evaluation score	87	2.62	0.43	1.50	3.00
Education and experience	87	43,739.53	8,054.30	28,014.00	54,799.00
Year-round schedule	87	0.29	0.46	0.00	1.00
Student level					
Reading pretest score	1,783	630.18	36.32	502.00	760.00
Reading posttest score	1,802	647.72	38.57	507.00	760.00
Math pretest score	1,803	607.95	31.62	456.00	740.00
Math posttest score	1,814	630.69	35.10	419.00	740.00
Composite pretest score	1,752	619.41	31.09	507.50	726.50
Composite posttest score	1,754	640.02	33.42	509.00	739.00
Female	1,947	0.51	0.50	0.00	1.00
Non-White	1,947	0.37	0.48	0.00	1.00
Special education	1,947	0.09	0.29	0.00	1.00
Free/Reduced-price lunch	1,947	0.35	0.48	0.00	1.00
Grade 5					
Teacher level					
Evaluation score	118	2.58	.44	1.10	3.00
Education and experience	118	43,628.51	8,369.83	28,014.00	54,799.00
Year-round schedule	118	0.31	0.47	0.00	1.00
Student level					
Reading pretest score	2,122	645.34	39.74	499.00	760.00
Reading posttest score	2,622	292.83	71.22	100.00	500.00
Math pretest score	2,131	628.77	33.49	419.00	740.00
Math posttest score	2,629	298.67	72.48	100.00	500.00
Composite pretest score	2,073	637.59	33.55	496.00	736.00
Composite posttest score	2,590	296.43	65.65	100.00	483.00
Female	2,755	0.47	0.50	0.00	1.00
Non-White	2,755	0.36	0.48	0.00	1.00
Special education	2,755	0.14	0.35	0.00	1.00
Free/Reduced-price lunch	2,755	0.35	0.48	0.00	1.00

Appendix C

Intercorrelations and Coefficient Alphas for Teacher Evaluation PC Scores, By Grade

	PC			
Teacher Evaluations	1	2	3	4
Grade 3				
PC 1	—			
PC 2	.708	—		
PC 3	.664	.657	—	
PC 4	.560	.617	.572	—
Grade 4				
PC 1	—			
PC 2	.764	—		
PC 3	.575	.628	—	
PC 4	.763	.692	.666	—
Grade 5				
PC 1	—			
PC 2	.857	—		
PC 3	.725	.765	—	
PC 4	.677	.662	.632	—

Note. PC = performance composite.
[a]a = .87. [b]a = .89. [c]a = .91.

Appendix D

Level 1 and Level 2 Results of Final Random Intercept Model

Variable	Third Grade			Fourth Grade			Fifth Grade		
	Coefficient	SE	p	Coefficient	SE	p	Coefficient	SE	p
Reading model									
Teacher level									
Evaluation score	4.74	5.51	.390	5.61	2.00	.005**	10.35	3.93	.009**
Education and experience	0.04	0.24	.858	0.05	0.11	.673	0.44	0.17	.010**
Year-round schedule	-4.50	3.78	.235	-5.64	1.90	.003**	-5.75	3.90	.140
Student level									
Pretest score	1.84	0.10	.000**	0.73	0.02	.000**	0.81	0.03	.000**
Female	9.35	2.18	.000**	1.37	0.98	.163	-0.30	1.79	.869
Non-White	-6.10	2.95	.038*	-2.79	1.22	.023*	-12.25	2.35	.000**
Special education	-26.9	4.18	.000**	-2.75	2.34	.240	-46.19	4.47	.000**
Free/Reduced-price lunch	-19.25	2.55	.000**	-3.66	1.32	.006**	-5.74	2.68	.032
Math model									
Teacher level									
Evaluation score	5.41	6.48	.404	1.73	2.14	.419	17.25	4.47	.000**
Education and experience	0.17	0.31	.580	-0.05	0.13	.706	0.48	0.19	.015*
Year-round schedule	-11.32	4.72	.017*	-7.49	2.02	.000**	-12.88	4.39	.004**
Student level									
Pretest score	2.33	0.13	.000**	0.72	0.03	.000**	0.93	0.04	.000**
Female	1.32	2.88	.646	0.43	0.98	.662	-6.10	1.85	.001**
Non-White	-10.15	3.30	.003	-0.06	1.36	.963	-10.66	2.69	.000**
Special education	-45.12	4.76	.000**	-4.69	2.54	.065	-48.40	3.91	.000**
Free/Reduced-price lunch	-19.45	3.11	.000**	-4.60	1.31	.001**	-9.56	2.87	.001**

(continued)

77

Appendix D (Continued)

Variable	Third Grade			Fourth Grade			Fifth Grade		
	Coefficient	SE	p	Coefficient	SE	p	Coefficient	SE	p
Combined reading and math model									
Teacher level									
Evaluation score	4.51	5.60	.421	3.51	1.85	.058	13.70	3.81	.001**
Education and experience	0.10	0.25	.685	0.03	0.11	.800	0.46	0.16	.004**
Year-round schedule	−6.67	3.90	.087	−6.86	1.71	.000**	−9.65	3.81	.012*
Student level									
Pretest score	2.32	0.13	.000**	0.74	0.02	.000**	0.93	0.034	.000**
Female	5.84	2.19	.008**	0.80	0.77	.297	−3.07	1.55	.047*
Non-White	−6.22	2.65	.019*	−0.25	1.00	.799	−9.83	2.14	.000**
Special education	−29.88	4.40	.000**	0.13	1.81	.942	−43.93	3.64	.000**
Free/Reduced-price lunch	−16.31	2.40	.000**	−3.88	1.15	.001**	−7.55	2.51	.003**

*p < .05. **p < .01.

PEABODY JOURNAL OF EDUCATION, 79(4), 79–107
Copyright © 2004, Lawrence Erlbaum Associates, Inc.

Vaughn Elementary's Innovative Teacher Evaluation System: Are Teacher Evaluation Scores Related to Growth in Student Achievement?

H. Alix Gallagher
Center for Education Policy
SRI International

In this study, I examined the validity of a performance-based, subject-specific teacher evaluation system by analyzing the relationship between teacher evaluation scores and student achievement. From a policy perspective, establishing validity was important because it is embedded in a knowledge-and skills-based pay system, which attached high stakes to evaluation scores.

In the first stage of the study, I used hierarchical linear modeling (HLM) to estimate value-added teacher effects, which were then correlated with teacher evaluation scores in literacy, mathematics, language arts, and a composite measure of student achievement. Additionally, teacher evaluation scores were

The research reported in this article was supported by a grant from the U.S. Department of Education, Office of Educational Research and Improvement, National Institute on Educational Governance, Finance, Policymaking, and Management to the Consortium for Policy Research in Education (CPRE) and the Wisconsin Center for Education Research, School of Education, University of Wisconsin–Madison (Grant OERI–R308A60003). The opinions expressed are those of the author and do not necessarily reflect the view of the National Institute on Educational Governance, Finance, Policymaking, and Management, Office of Educational Research and Improvement, U.S. Department of Education; the institutional partners of CPRE; or the Wisconsin Center for Education Research.

Requests for reprints should be sent to H. Alix Gallagher, SRI International, Center for Education Policy, 333 Ravenswood Avenue, BS Third Floor, Menlo Park, CA 94025. E-mail: alix.gallagher@sri.com inserted into the HLM models as subject-specific predictors of student achievement. Results indicate a strong, positive, and statistically significant relationship between teacher evaluation scores and student achievement in reading and a composite measure of teacher and student performance and a positive, although not statistically significant, relationship in mathematics.

In the second stage of the study, I used document analyses and interviews with teachers to explore factors affecting the relationship between teacher evaluation scores and student achievement across subjects. Findings suggest that the relationship is stronger in reading than mathematics because both teachers and evaluators have more pedagogical knowledge and better alignment to standards and assessments in reading than in math.

As schools and districts across the country work to improve student achievement, it is important that high-quality teaching and high-quality teachers be identified. To determine the effects of high-quality teaching, a valid and reliable method of identifying quality instruction is necessary. Yet previous research has shown that traditional principal evaluations of teachers are inadequate both for differentiating between more and less proficient teachers and as a basis for guiding improvements in teaching skills (Danielson, 1996; Medley & Coker, 1987; Peterson, 2000). In this article, I examine the relationship between teacher evaluation scores (TES) from a new, performance-based assessment system and value-added measures of student achievement. Hierarchical linear modeling (HLM) is used to isolate classroom effects, which are the growth in student achievement attributable to the group effect of having a particular teacher after controlling for individual student characteristics including student achievement. In a valid teacher evaluation system, the relationship between TES and value-added learning growth (classroom effects) should be strong, although not total because some desired but noninstructional characteristics of teachers (e.g., record keeping, participation in school governance) might be only distantly related to student achievement in the short term.

Specifically, in the study I examined the relationship between TES and student achievement at Vaughn Elementary School, which is implementing both an innovative teacher evaluation and knowledge- and skills-based pay system. In the study, I first estimated classroom effects in four subject areas. Next, I calculated the correlation between classroom effects and TES. Then I tested TES and teacher characteristics (certification and years of experience) as alternative, Level 2 predictors of variation in student achievement. Finally, in a qualitative component, I examined factors that contributed to the strength of the relationship between TES and student outcomes in literacy in contrast with mathematics.

Policy and Theoretical Background

The main goal of standards-based reform is to improve student outcomes by focusing on student achievement. Many researchers and policymakers have noted that to improve student learning, teachers will need to increase their skills (Corcoran, 1995; Darling-Hammond, 1999; Darling-Hammond & McLaughlin, 1995). One strategy advanced for motivating teachers to acquire the capacity necessary to achieve the goals of standards-based reform is knowledge- and skills-based pay, which provides financial rewards to teachers who improve their instructional expertise toward a set of teaching standards (Odden & Kelley, 2002). The effectiveness of such a system rests on implementation and also on the validity of the teacher evaluation system on which the rewards are based. In this study, I utilized extant research to develop a theoretical framework about how TES would be related to student achievement in a valid teacher evaluation system.

For this study, I drew from four interrelated bodies of literature:

1. Studies of traditional teacher evaluation systems, which show that they have little or no connection to student learning gains.
2. Examinations of new, performance-based teacher evaluations designed to improve instructional practice and enhance student learning.
3. Recent classroom effects research that shows teachers have major impacts on student learning gains. (This research is often referred to as teacher effects research. The term *classroom effects* is used here because it more accurately describes group effects after controlling for certain student and teacher characteristics.)
4. Research on effective teaching, which shows that teachers' pedagogical content knowledge can help teachers boost student learning of complex material.

Most previous studies of teacher evaluation have shown that typical evaluations are seen by both teachers and principals as having little value and that principals' ratings of teachers generally are uncorrelated with student achievement (Medley & Coker, 1987; Peterson, 2000). Studies in the private sector suggest that this is partly because it is desirable to evaluate employees on some skills that have only indirect connections to measurable outcomes; however, principals' evaluations of teachers generally have a much weaker correlation with outcomes than supervisory ratings in other fields (Heneman, 1986).

Recent innovations in teacher evaluation, however, have suggested that evaluations that are subject specific and use multiple sources of data could lead to substantial improvements in the validity of teacher evaluation systems (Danielson, 1996; Porter, Youngs, & Odden, 2001). The goal of this study was to investigate an innovative teacher evaluation system at Vaughn Elementary School to examine the link between TES and classroom-level variation in value-added student achievement (i.e., classroom effects).

The investigation of the validity of the teacher evaluation system was premised on a substantial research base on classroom effects. Unlike early research on school and classroom effects that found that student characteristics were the largest determinants of student achievement (Coleman, 1990), more recent work has utilized more advanced statistical techniques (frequently HLM) to show that teachers and schools have substantial effects on student outcomes (Darling-Hammond, 2000; Du & Heistad, 1999; Haycock, 1998; Heistad, 1999; Mendro, 1998; Meyer, 1996a, 1996b, 1997; Rowan, 1999, 2001; Webster & Mendro, 1997; Wright, Horn, & Sanders, 1997). Once such classroom effects were found at Vaughn, it became possible to examine the relationship between TES and student achievement to assess the validity of the evaluation system.

For both theoretical and practical reasons, it was also desirable to identify the factors that led to the strength or weakness of the relationship between TES and classroom effects across subjects. To this end, relevant literature was used to build a framework for a qualitative study around key concepts of teacher knowledge and instructional expertise and factors likely to mediate the relationship between TES and student achievement. Literature on high-quality teaching was reviewed; this review showed that the concept of pedagogical content knowledge could be used to describe several facets of effective teaching for understanding. Pedagogical content knowledge is teachers' understanding of content and how to teach it including typical student misconceptions and strategies for helping students overcome them (Bransford, Brown, & Cocking, 1999; Shulman, 1987). Grossman's (1990) expansion of this concept into four components (knowledge of purposes for teaching subject matter, knowledge of students' understanding, knowledge of curricular and instructional materials, and knowledge of instructional strategies) was used as a framework for exploring teacher quality in the second part of the study.

Past research on teacher efficacy has suggested that the combination of teachers' expectations for their students and for themselves could have an important influence on student outcomes that would not necessarily be picked up by an evaluation system that addressed teachers' knowledge and skills (Ashton & Webb, 1986; Dembo & Gibson, 1985; Lumpe, Haney, &

Czerniak, 2000; Ross, 1998; Soodak & Podell, 1998; Tschannen-Moran, Hoy, & Hoy, 1998). Porter and Smithson's (2000a, 2000b) work on alignment of enacted and tested curriculum showed that the alignment of the content teachers taught to the student achievement test (Stanford Achievement Test, 9th ed. [SAT–9]) could also mediate the relationship between TES and student achievement.

Combined, the reviewed literature was used to build the theoretical framework for the study. Previous research has suggested that there is a definite causal connection between teacher knowledge and skills and student learning, which can be mediated by teacher efficacy and curricular alignment. In the study, I examined the relationship between measures of teacher knowledge and skill (TES), mediating factors (efficacy and alignment), and measures of student learning (classroom effects). Figure 1 shows the theoretical framework.

Vaughn Elementary was chosen as the site for the study because it was in its 3rd year of implementing an innovative teacher evaluation system that is based on a complex understanding of high-quality teaching, is subject specific, and has multiple sources of data for evaluation. Past research (Kellor, Milanowski, Odden, & Gallagher, 2001; Milanowski & Gallagher, 2001) has also suggested that the system was well implemented.

Site Description

Vaughn Elementary is a charter school in the Los Angeles Unified School District (LAUSD) serving approximately 1,200 students. The school is 100% Title 1 and 100% free/reduced lunch; 85% of its student body is classified as English language learners. Prior to receiving a charter in 1993, Vaughn had very low student achievement, with many students scoring in the lowest 10th percentile on norm-referenced tests. In its charter, Vaughn listed improving student performance as a critical goal and measure of

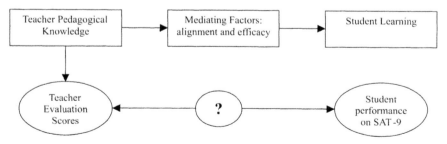

Figure 1. Theoretical framework.

83

success. Student performance has improved substantially since obtaining charter status, and the school has been recognized as a National Blue Ribbon School and has qualified for a school performance bonus under the California Academic Performance Index (a measure of school performance in the state accountability system) during the 1999–2000 school year (Milanowski & Gallagher, 2001; WestEd, 1998).

To improve student achievement, Vaughn designed an innovative teacher evaluation process linked to knowledge- and skills-based pay. The core of the system is teacher standards, which were designed by the Vaughn staff to represent its view of high-quality teaching in significant detail. The Vaughn teacher evaluation is based on a subject-specific adaptation of the Danielson (1996) Framework for Teaching. This means that teachers are evaluated using rubrics that describe a level of proficiency for each of up to nine standards within each of 10 domains, 7 of which are subject specific (see Gallagher, 2002, for the rubrics). Vaughn's Teacher Assistance and Review Standards Matrix (referred to here as the Vaughn rubrics) are used simultaneously for formative and summative assessment. Based on results, teachers are referred for professional development opportunities in areas identified as weaknesses; teachers also receive financial rewards based on their scores. At the most basic level, the goal of the system is to focus teachers on a school-developed vision of high-quality teaching and to thereby improve student performance. In the remainder of this section, I describe the evaluation and rewards system in greater detail and show why Vaughn has a theoretically high-quality teacher evaluation system.

For evaluation purposes, Vaughn categorized teachers into three groups:

- Salary Category 1: Teachers working toward full California teaching credential.
- Salary Category 2: Fully licensed teachers who have achieved an average rating of 3.0 (proficient) in all five basic areas.
- Salary Category 3: Fully licensed expert teachers whose average score across all domains is at least a 3.5.

Teachers in the first category were evaluated on fewer domains, although the evaluation process was the same.

Evaluations began with a preconference in which the teacher and evaluator discussed the curriculum and instruction in the teachers' classroom. This gave the teacher an opportunity to discuss any contextual factors of which the observer might not be aware. In addition, observers could address any teacher questions about the process.

During the evaluation week, evaluators observed the teacher teaching each major content area in which she or he was being evaluated. Although these visits were officially unscheduled, at times teachers and evaluators needed to communicate about when teachers would teach a given subject so that the evaluator could be present to observe. Evaluators used teaching observations, lesson plans, student work, and any other relevant documentation about curricular and instructional strategies to assess teachers. Although student work and portfolios were sometimes used to document all aspects of a teacher's practice, no formal evaluation of student achievement is part of the teacher evaluation system.

At the conclusion of each evaluation cycle, evaluators met with the teacher to discuss the evaluation, provide feedback, and answer questions from the teacher. The postconference also enabled teachers to explain anything that was unclear to the observer and to provide additional documentation of competencies if necessary.

This preconference and postconference system was developed during the 2000–01 school year to reduce the stress from the evaluation process and increase observers' knowledge of the teachers' classrooms and thus the perceived accuracy of teacher ratings. It was also intended to increase the amount of feedback that teachers receive and thus move the evaluation process from one geared largely toward summative evaluation to one that teachers perceive as an opportunity for growth, even though it carries high stakes (Milanowski & Gallagher, 2001).

The Vaughn rubrics recognize the importance of students' opportunity to learn material in predicting student outcomes. For example, the mathematics rubrics recognize five strands of mathematical concepts (number sense, algebra/functions, measurement and geometry, statistics/data analysis and probability, and math reasoning), which are similar to the state's mathematics content standards. To receive an exemplary score, teachers need to provide balanced instruction in all areas. This standard evaluates whether teachers cover all major areas in the California student standards.

The Vaughn evaluation system is content specific and attempts to evaluate pedagogical content knowledge. Although the rubrics do not give any indication that teachers need to be aware of misconceptions that students are likely to have about a content or skill area, the rubrics indicate the importance of ongoing assessment of student progress. In addition, the rubrics recognize different skills and strategies for each content area and the appropriateness of different instructional materials for different learning situations. Although this is not a comprehensive evaluation of teachers' pedagogical content knowledge, it is potentially sufficient as a rough proxy. As I discuss later, the information about pedagogical content knowledge supplied by the rubric was supplemented by interview data.

Each domain is disaggregated into between two and nine different standards on which each teacher is rated on a scale ranging from 1 (*unsatisfactory*) to 4 (*exemplary*) based on a rubric that describes behaviors that indicate competency levels. Scores from each evaluator were averaged to form a score for each domain. Scores for each domain were then averaged to create an overall score. All domains were weighted equally.

There were 10 domains that teachers could have been evaluated on:

1. Lesson planning (all teachers).
2. Classroom management (all teachers).
3. Literacy (all teachers).
4. Language development (including oral language, language usage, English as a second language, and sheltered English; all teachers).
5. Mathematics (all teachers).
6. Special education inclusion (all teachers who have special education students).
7. History and social sciences (Salary Category 2 and 3 teachers).
8. Science (Salary Category 2 and 3 teachers).
9. The arts (Salary Category 2 and 3 teachers).
10. Technology (Salary Category 2 and 3 teachers).

In addition, teachers can receive a bonus for being certified in the specialty area of bilingual education. For the 2000–01 school year, teachers were evaluated at least three times. (Some chose to be evaluated for a fourth time.) Each evaluation included a self-evaluation and classroom observations in all subjects by a trained peer evaluator and a trained administrative evaluator based on the Vaughn rubrics. Peer, administrator, and self-evaluations were weighted evenly. Observations were made during three (or four) 1-week windows during the year.

The evaluation and knowledge- and skills-based pay system was designed to improve the quality of teachers already at Vaughn by providing a more accurate assessment of teachers' skills than typical evaluation systems. In addition, it is seen as a recruitment advantage because depending on their evaluation scores, new teachers (as well as experienced teachers) can earn more pay at Vaughn than they could at nearby schools. Furthermore, it focuses teachers on the school's teaching standards through a comprehensive evaluation process with up to over $13,000 per teacher in pay tied to performance. Results of past teacher surveys and interviews conducted by the Consortium for Policy Research in Education indicate that increasing student achievement is perceived as a key school goal and that this focus on student achievement is one of the most important reasons teachers want to work at Vaughn (Kellor et al., 2001). This provides evidence that the substantial extrinsic rewards symbolize a school-wide commitment to student learning.

Results from the 2001 Vaughn Annual Performance Pay Survey (Milanowski & Gallagher, 2001) indicate that the system is motivating teachers to improve their skills. Responses indicate that 90.9% of teachers feel they can achieve a proficient rating on the standards, 86.6% made a great effort to develop the skills and knowledge rewarded by the system, and 75.0% found that the financial rewards were large enough to motivate them to develop the skills and knowledge. These percentages reinforce the notion that extrinsic rewards do not inherently conflict with teachers' intrinsic motivation.

The evaluation process embedded in Vaughn's knowledge- and skills-based pay system includes many of the recommendations for improving the quality of teacher evaluation. It contains an understanding of teaching as a cognitively complex activity; it uses multiple sources of data on teacher performance, has a content-specific understanding of high-quality teaching, and uses multiple evaluators. However, it does not include measures of student achievement as evaluative criteria. As a result, given the high stakes attached to the evaluation results, in this study, I sought to explore whether the Vaughn system has predictive validity.

Methods

Once the theoretical framework was developed, a two-part research design was conceived: (a) a quantitative part to measure the statistical relationship between TES and classroom effects and (b) a qualitative part to triangulate these results with an understanding of teachers' and evaluators' pedagogical content knowledge and the influence of mediating factors.

Quantitative

The sample for the quantitative part of the study was the population of Vaughn's second- through fifth-grade teachers ($n = 34$) and all students in their classrooms with available pretest and posttest data ($n = 584$ for reading and math, $n = 532$ for language arts, $n = 527$ for composite). Prior to conducting the quantitative analysis, teacher evaluation data were analyzed for interrater reliability both through the computation of a coefficient alpha and an analysis of percent of rater agreement. Table 1 shows that there was relatively high interrater reliability in TES. In the study I proceeded next to the core statistical models.

Table 1

Reliability of Teacher Evaluation System

Evaluation Domain	Alpha Coefficient	% All Evaluator Ratings Within 0.5	% All Evaluator Ratings Within 1.0
Literacy	.81	63	92
Mathematics	.83	57	92
Language arts	.83	67	90
Lesson planning	.81	69	96
Classroom management	.76	59	92
Core five areas (average of the above areas)	.86	80	94

The core analyses used value-added methodology to address four main questions about the population of Vaughn's second- through fifth-grade classrooms while controlling for differences in student characteristics. These characteristics include attendance, English proficiency, gender, parental educational attainment (this was not available for fifth-grade students because they had graduated and the LAUSD data system did not allow Vaughn to access student data once students left the school), retention the previous year, special education placement, and grade level and prior achievement (SAT–9 scores in reading, mathematics, and language arts from spring 2000 testing). A measure of poverty was not included because the population was homogenous. Table 2 presents descriptions of all Level 1 variables. Table 3 presents all Level 2 variables. Value-added HLM models were used because they provide more accurate estimates of the error structure of the data (in that they take into account the nested and nonindependent nature of the data) and can be used to control for student characteristics (Bryk & Raudenbush, 1992; Snijders & Bosker, 1999). As a result, value-added HLM models are well suited for identifying the effects of teachers or schools on student achievement, which was the goal of this study.

The basic structure of an HLM model for a classroom value-added analysis has two levels and can be represented as follows:

$$\text{Level 1: } Y_{ij} = \beta_{0j} + \beta_{1j}X_{1ij} + \beta_{2j}X_{2ij} + \ldots + \beta_{kj}X_{kij} + r_{ij}$$

$$\text{Level 2: } \beta_{0j} = \gamma_{00} + \gamma_{01}W_j + U_{0j}$$
$$\beta_{1j} = \gamma_{10}$$
$$\beta_{kj} = \gamma_{k0}$$

Level 1 is the student level where Y_{ij} is the dependent variable and represents a posttest score, β_{0j} is the intercept and equals the average

Table 2

Level 1 Variables

Student Characteristic	Measure	M	SD
Poverty	Participation in free and reduced lunch or Title 1; not included, as all students qualify for both.		NA
English proficiency	English Language Development Scale rating. This was split to		
	Beginning (Level 1–2)	0.07	0.26
	Emergent (Level 3–4, which was the reference group)	0.21	0.41
	Proficient (Level 5–6)	0.23	0.42
	Missing data were imputed based on class mean English language development.		
Parental educational attainment	Parental reporting. After exploratory analyses, this was split to		
	Less than high school	0.39	0.49
	High school or beyond (reference group)	0.34	0.47
	Missing data were denoted with a dummy variable.		
Participation in special education	Whether students have testing accommodations	0.04	0.19
Retention in the previous year	Whether students took the same grade level assessment in both 2000 and 2001	0.06	0.23
Grade level	Student grade level in both 2000 and 2001	NA	
	Percentages are presented for 2001:		
	Second grade	26%	
	Third grade	28%	
	Fourth grade	26%	
	Fifth grade	20%	
Student race/ethnicity	Student designated ethnicity category; not included due to homogeneity		
Gender	Student designated gender category	0.51	0.50
Attendance	Number of days present during 2000–01 school year (out of 180 possible days)	174.23	8.82
	Missing data were imputed using school mean and were denoted with a dummy variable	0.01	0.09
Reading in 2000	SAT–9 scale score	564.26	48.34
	Missing data were imputed using mean imputation for the grade level and was denoted with a dummy variable)	0.07	0.26
Math in 2000	SAT–9 scale score	574.61	43.47
Language Arts in 2000	SAT–9 scale score	579.58	37.08
Composite in 2000	Average of three SAT–9 scale scores	605.42	36.61
Reading in 2001	SAT–9 scale score	597.97	41.05
Math in 2001	SAT–9 scale score	610.74	40.65
Language Arts in 2001	SAT–9 scale score	601.99	37.91
Composite in 2001	Average of three SAT–9 scale scores	605.42	36.61

Note.   NA = not applicable; SAT–9 = Stanford Achievement Test, 9th edition.

Table 3

Level 2 Variables

Variable	Description	M	SD
Years of experience	Scale variable, which was also converted into dummy variables for ≤ 2 years, ≥ 5 years, and > 5 years (3–4 years as a reference group)	5.57	5.26
Certification	Dummy variable for whether teachers had a clear credential (full certification); also a dummy variable for whether teachers had a bilingual endorsement (BCLAD)	0.53	0.51
Teacher salary category in Vaughn system	Scale variable (1–3), which was converted into a dummy variable for whether someone was Salary Category 2 or 3	0.50	0.51
Average classroom English language development level	Continuous variable (1.0–6.0)	3.78	0.79
Average lesson planning TES	Scale variable (1.0–4.0)	3.27	0.57
Average classroom management TES	Scale variable (1.0–4.0)	3.36	0.49
Average literacy TES	Scale variable (1.0–4.0)	3.24	0.39
Average mathematics TES	Scale variable (1.0–4.0)	3.13	0.42
Average language TES	Scale variable (1.0–4.0)	3.24	0.42
Average across the five core areas listed above	Continuous variable (1.0–4.0)	3.25	0.42
Average across all domains	Continuous variable (1.0–4.0)	3.20	0.39

Note. BCLAD = Bilingual Crosscultural, Language and Academic Development certificate; TES = teacher evaluation scores.

growth in student achievement in classroom j controlling for student characteristics, β_{1j} is the coefficient for effect of the pretest score on posttest score, β_{kj} is the coefficient for the effect of student characteristics on posttest score, and r_{ij} is the error term. Level 2 is the classroom level where β_{kj} are independent variables, W_j are second-level predictor variables, γ_{00} is the average classroom intercept for the population of classrooms, β_{01} is the effect of classroom conditions on achievement, γ_{10} is the average classroom slope of pretest on posttest, γ_{k0} is the average classroom slope of characteristics, and U_{0j} is the unique effect of classroom j on mean achievement holding W_j constant. In these analyses, classroom effects were estimated using the empirical Bayes estimates of the residuals of U_{0j}. The value-added analyses separately explored the relationships between TES and classroom effects across reading, math, language arts, and a composite measure of academic performance. For each, four key questions were answered.

The first question is, what is the average student achievement growth (the term *growth* is used here to connote the residualized gain from pre-test to posttest) in each class? This was addressed using the following model:

Model 1

$$\text{Level 1: Posttest}_{ij} = \beta_{0j} + \theta\text{Pretest}_{ij} + \alpha\text{studchar}_{ij} + r_{ij}$$

$$\text{Level 2: } \beta_{0j} = \gamma_{00} + U_{0j}$$
$$\beta_{kj} = \gamma_{k0}$$

Empirical Bayes estimates for U_{0j}, the random effects of different class-rooms, were derived from this model using HLM and SPSS (Version 11.0). Empirical Bayes estimates describe the difference from the overall, or pre-dicted, level for a given variable. They were preferable to ordinary least squares estimates of residuals for this study because they have shrinkage, which increases the reliability of the estimates by more heavily weighting more reliable data (Bryk & Raudenbush, 1992; Snijders & Bosker, 1999). This conservative estimate of classroom effects was especially desirable due to the varying sample sizes across classrooms. The empirical Bayes es-timates were used to identify individual classroom effects on student achievement.

The random intercept model just listed, which is statistically identical to a random effects analysis of covariance (ANCOVA) model, is also advanta-geous because it provides information about the percentage of variation in outcomes at the two levels. This can be calculated using the intraclass cor-relation coefficient, represented as: $\rho = \tau_{00}/(\tau_{00} + \sigma^2)$. The models employed in all the remaining analyses were also random intercept models. Random slope models were also explored, but due potentially to the relatively small sample size, no significant variation in slopes was detected.

The second question is, how does the Vaughn measure of teacher qual-ity correlate with classroom effects identified in Model 1? To answer this, a correlation analysis was conducted for each subject area between TES and empirical Bayes estimates of classrooms' student performance. This corre-lation analysis enabled comparison to previous research in the human re-sources field, which examined evaluation validity using correlations be-tween measurable employee outcomes and evaluation scores.

The third question is, are Vaughn's TES statistically significant predic-tors of classroom variation in student achievement? This was assessed by inserting TES into the second level of the HLM model as a predictor of vari-ation in student achievement.

Model 2

$$\text{Level 1: Posttest}_{ij} = \beta_{0j} + \theta\text{Pretest}_{ij} + \alpha\text{studchar}_{ij} + r_{ij}$$

$$\text{Level 2: } \beta_{0j} = \gamma_{00} + \gamma_{01}(\text{TES})_j + U_{0j}$$
$$\beta_{kj} = \gamma_{k0} + \gamma_{k1}W_j$$

If TES were found to be significant and positive, this would indicate that the evaluation score was succeeding in predicting variations in student outcomes. Results from the correlation of TES and classroom effects and the use of TES as a Level 2 predictor should be similar.

In addition, by comparing the τ_{00} estimates from the random intercept model and the model with Level 2 predictors (pred.), it is possible to determine the proportion of variance explained (Prop of Var expl.) by the Level 2 (L2) predictor using the equation

Prop of Var expl. L2 = $\hat{\tau}_{00}$(random ANCOVA) − $\hat{\tau}_{00}$ (Level 2 pred. Model)] / $\hat{\tau}_{00}$(random ANCOVA).

This equation is applicable only to models that are identical at Level 1 but use alternate predictors at Level 2. This enabled comparisons of the effectiveness of different teacher evaluation elements in explaining variation in student achievement.

The fourth question relates this study to prior research on teacher characteristics: Do teacher characteristics, such as licensure and years of experience, predict variation in student achievement? Data were collected on teachers' licensure status, years of experience, and master's degrees. Master's degrees had to be dropped from this study due to lack of variation. However, both licensure status and years of experience were entered separately into the second level of the model to assess whether those widely collected teacher characteristics predicted variation in student achievement.

Model 3

$$\text{Level 1: Posttest}_{ij} = \beta_{0j} + \theta\text{Pretest}_{ij} + \alpha\text{studchar}_{ij} + \varepsilon_{ij}$$

$$\text{Level 2: } \beta_{0j} = \gamma_{00} + \gamma_{01}(\text{licensure})_j + \gamma_{02}(\text{years of experience})_j + U_{0j}$$
$$\beta_{kj} = \gamma_{k0} + \gamma_{k1}W_j$$

A model that used both TES and teacher characteristics was also explored; however, it proved unfruitful because the small sample size provided few degrees of freedom for the analysis.

Each of these analyses was run for reading, math, language arts, and a composite performance model for a total of 16 core analyses. Taken as a whole, the results would show the relationship between teacher quality (as measured by the Vaughn teacher evaluation system and traditionally collected teacher characteristics) and student achievement.

Qualitative

In the second part of the study, I explored how several factors influenced the strength of the relationship between TES and classroom effects in two key subjects: literacy and mathematics. Based on the relevant literature, teachers' pedagogical content knowledge, sense of efficacy, and alignment of instruction to the SAT–9 and California state standards were explored through document analyses and interviews. Questions on pedagogical content knowledge covered its four key domains: knowledge of purposes of instruction, knowledge of students, knowledge of curricular and instructional materials, and knowledge of instructional strategies. In the next section, I describe how the interview sample was developed.

To gain a better understanding of the evaluation process and the role of pedagogical content knowledge in the teacher evaluation system, both teachers and evaluators were interviewed. For the teacher sample, six teachers were selected for each subject. Teachers who were outliers were selected to facilitate comparisons between pedagogical content knowledge, alignment, and efficacy of teachers in three groups:

1. High classroom effects but low TES.
2. Low classroom effects but high TES.
3. High classroom effects and high TES.

In a sense, the third group of teachers represented the desired outcome from the evaluation system, whereas the other groups provided contrasts that could potentially explain factors that led to a stronger or weaker relationship between evaluation scores and classroom effects.

Evaluators were selected for their ability to provide insights into the evaluation process in the grades being studied. Both administrative evaluators who evaluated second- through fifth-grade teachers were interviewed. In addition, one peer evaluator was interviewed in her role as a peer evaluator; four other peer evaluators were interviewed as part of the teacher sample.

The methodology used in this study required a trade-off. Although the small sample size limits generalizability, the in-depth qualitative study of one school's innovative teacher evaluation system allowed me as the researcher to explore factors that led to greater or lesser predictive validity across subjects, thus providing explanations of the quantitative findings. The in-depth focus on one school facilitated important contributions to the growing understanding of how to improve the validity and utility of teacher evaluation systems.

Summary of Results of Quantitative Component

To address the first question, value-added HLM models of subject-specific (reading, math, and language arts) and overall performance were utilized (with no Level 2 predictors). In preliminary analyses, gender (Level 1), average classroom pretest (Level 2), and average classroom English language development (ELD; Level 2) were explored. They were dropped from the final analyses because they were not important theoretically and were statistically insignificant.

Both reading and math scores from the spring 2000 testing were included in the model to increase the reliability of the understanding of students' prior performance. The model used for reading is presented along with the results (GC = grand centered):

$$\text{Level 1: ScaledReading01} = \beta_0 + \beta_1(\text{GCAttendance})_{ij} +$$
$$\beta_2(\text{ImputeAttendance})_{ij} + \beta_3(\text{Retain})_{ij} + \beta_4(\text{SpecialEducation})_{ij} +$$
$$\beta_5(\text{GC ScaledReading00})_{ij} + \beta_6(\text{GCScaledMath00})_{ij} +$$
$$\beta_7(\text{ImputedReading})_{ij} + \beta_8(\text{ImputedELD})_{ij} + \beta_9(\text{EarlyELD})_{ij} +$$
$$\beta_{10}(\text{EnglishProficient})_{ij} + \beta_{11}(\text{ParentsNoHS})_{ij} + \beta_{12}(\text{MissingParentEd})_{ij} +$$
$$\beta_{13}(\text{Grade 3})_{ij} + \beta_{14}(\text{Grade 4})_{ij} + \beta_{15}(\text{Grade 5})_{ij} + R_{ij}$$

$$\text{Level 2: } \beta_0 = \gamma_{00} + U_{0j}$$
$$\beta_1 \text{ through } \beta_{15} \text{ are fixed.}$$

In this model, β_0 can be interpreted as the average growth in test score for the average student. This referred to a student who was present 174 days (the GC mean attendance), was not retained the previous year, was not in special education, was an intermediate English language learner, had at least one parent graduate from high school, had no missing or imputed data, and received an average score on reading and math tests in 2000 controlling for grade level. Grade-level control variables are important because grade levels were combined in this study, and previous research has shown that student gains on achievement tests may slow in the upper grades and best practices in curriculum and instruction vary across grades (Du & Heistad, 1999). The latter issue could lead to systematic variation in teacher evaluation across grade levels if the evaluation system is not sensitive to such differences. U_{0j} is the classroom-specific value-added effect, with g_{00} representing the average growth for the average student. R_{ij} is the individual deviation from the predicted gain that is not attributable to the classroom effect. The interpretation of the variables was similar in subsequent models.

The results of the random intercept model used to generate the empirical Bayes estimates are presented in Table 4. Similar models were run for mathematics, language arts, and the composite. The Level 1 results for other subjects are not reported here, because the Level 1 variables serve solely as controls for the variables of theoretical interest. Full results and interpretation for all models and all levels are presented in Gallagher (2002). Level 2 results from all random intercept models are presented next. Chi-square tests for differences in intercepts across groups were statistically significant in all four types of models. Table 5 reports the percentage of variation located at Level 2 (intraclass correlation coefficient ρ) in the four areas as well as the reliability of β_0. These results can be interpreted in three ways that have importance for this study and research on classroom effects. First, there are significant classroom effects at Vaughn. Second, the effects are smallest in reading, potentially indicating that

Table 4

Results for the Random Intercept Model for Reading

Fixed Effect	Coefficient	SE	t ratio	p
Intercept G00	601.75	4.09	147.09	0.000**
Attendance (grand centered) G10	−0.01	0.09	−0.114	0.91
Impute attendance G20	6.59	8.91	0.74	0.46
Retain G30	−9.52	3.51	−2.72	0.01*
Special education G40	−23.53	4.27	−5.51	0.00**
Scaled reading pretest (grand centered) G50	0.55	0.04	15.42	0.00**
Scaled math pretest (grand centered) G60	0.20	0.03	6.07	0.00**
Impute reading G70	−1.92	3.60	−0.53	0.59
Impute ELD G80	−3.06	2.45	−1.25	0.21
Beginning ELD G90	−7.79	3.93	−1.98	0.05*
English proficient G100	5.52	2.74	2.01	0.04*
Parent no high school G110	−1.51	2.06	−0.73	0.47
Missing parent education G120	−2.86	2.94	−0.97	0.33
Grade 3 G130	−0.21	4.95	−0.04	0.97
Grade 4 G140	1.43	5.33	0.27	0.79
Grade 5 G150	−5.64	6.84	−0.82	0.41

Note. G refers to γ. Reliability of $\beta_0 = 0.79$; $\tau_{00} = 80.93$, chi-square $p = 0.000$; $\sigma^2 = 361.95$; $\rho = .18$. Scale is a 1-point gain in reading on the spring 2001 test. ELD = English language development.

*$p < .05$. **$p < .001$.

Table 5

Intraclass Correlation Coefficient Across Subjects

	Reading	Mathematics	Language Arts	Composite
ρ	.18	.23	.22	.27
Reliability of β_0	.79	.83	.81	.84

Table 6

Correlation Between Classroom Effects and Teacher Evaluation Scores Across Subjects

Reading	Mathematics	Language Arts	Composite
.50**	.21	.18	.36*

$*p = .05$, two-tailed. $**p = .01$, two-tailed.

teaching at Vaughn (in terms of effectiveness and alignment) is less varied across classrooms in reading than in other subjects. Finally, this finding could also be interpreted to support earlier research that has shown smaller classroom effects in reading due to home instruction in reading (Entwisle, Alexander, & Olson, 1997; Hanushek, Kain, & Rivkin, 1998).

Once the existence of statistically different classroom effects was confirmed in each subject, the correlation between classroom effects (empirical Bayes estimates of U_0) and TES in each subject was calculated and are presented in Table 6. The correlation between TES in literacy and classroom effects in reading was both statistically significant and very high compared to other previous literature on evaluation both within education and in the private sector (Heneman, 1986; Medley & Coker, 1987; Peterson, 2000). The degree of association was somewhat surprising because both the standard deviation of TES (0.39) and the intraclass correlation coefficient (.18) were smaller in literacy than any other subject. The significance of the composite score is also important from the perspective of Vaughn policy because teachers move between salary categories (1, 2, and 3) largely on the basis of their composite evaluation score. Movement from Salary Category 1 to 2 also requires obtaining full certification. It is worth noting, however, that the significance of the composite score can be partially attributed to the strength of the correlation in one component of the composite: in this case, literacy.

The third question from the quantitative stage of the analysis was how well the teacher evaluation scores predicted variation in classroom effects, that is, value-added learning growth. To answer this question, subject-specific teacher evaluation scores were inserted into Level 2 of the HLM models. This question was examined using the following model, which is identical to the random intercept model used earlier with the exception of the addition of the teachers' literacy evaluation scores at Level 2:

Level 1: $Y = \beta_0 + \beta_1(\text{GCAttendance})_{ij} + \beta_2(\text{ImputeAttendance})_{ij} + \beta_3(\text{Retain})_{ij} + \beta_4(\text{SpecialEducation})_{ij} + \beta_5(\text{GCScaledReading00})_{ij} + \beta_6(\text{GCScaledMath00})_{ij} + \beta_7(\text{ImputedReading})_{ij} + \beta_8(\text{ImputedELD})_{ij} + \beta_9(\text{EarlyELD})_{ij} + \beta_{10}(\text{EnglishProficient})_{ij} + \beta_{11}(\text{ParentsNoHS})_{ij} + \beta_{12}(\text{MissingParentEd})_{ij} + \beta_{13}(\text{Grade 3})_{ij} + \beta_{14}(\text{Grade 4})_{ij} + \beta_{15}(\text{Grade 5})_{ij} + R_{ij}$

Level 2: $\beta_0 = \gamma_{00} + (\text{AvgLiteracyTES}) + U_{0j}$
β_1 through β_{15} are fixed.[1]

Results are presented in Table 7.

The most important finding for this analysis is that teachers' average evaluation scores in literacy were a highly statistically significant predictor of student performance. For every point increase in TES, student performance increased about 14 points.

Perhaps a more useful way to look at this, given the relatively small variation in teacher evaluation scores in reading, is to note that for every standard deviation of improvement in literacy teacher evaluation score ($0.39 = 1\ SD$), student performance improved 5.53 points. The range in teachers' evaluation scores in literacy was 1.55 points, so the difference in growth in student achievement for the top performing class and the bottom performing class, after controlling for all other factors, was predicted to be 21.98 points a year. This represents slightly less than two thirds of the average growth in reading for Vaughn students from 2000 to 2001 and was thus a practically significant result.[2]

Another way to look at the effectiveness of the literacy TES is to see how much of the between-class variation in student achievement that was rep-

[1]Models with multiple evaluation scores, including lesson planning and classroom management, entered as Level 2 predictors were also explored. Potentially due to the small sample size and high correlation among the evaluation scores, these did not appear to be reliable because the coefficients for Level 2 predictors switched seemingly randomly from positive to negative when additional variables were added, and p values were far from significant (e.g., $p = .873$ for classroom management when entered into the preceding literacy model). As a result, only models with one evaluation score at Level 2 are reported.

[2]Harcourt Brace, the publisher of the SAT–9, would not release norms and reliability information about the California form of the SAT–9, so I could not compare growth in scale scores of students at Vaughn to a sample that was representative of either the nation or the state of California. However, because Vaughn's average National Percentile Rank is approximately 38th percentile schoolwide, 1 year of growth at Vaughn is probably slightly less than one grade-level equivalent on national norms.

Table 7

Literacy TES as a Predictor of Student Performance in Reading

Fixed Effect	Coefficient	SE	t ratio	p
Intercept G0	558.66	13.34	41.88	.00***
Average literacy TES (grand centered) G01	14.18	4.19	3.39	.00***
Attendance (grand centered) G10	−0.03	0.09	−0.30	.77
Impute attendance G20	6.71	8.89	0.76	.45
Retain G30	−9.23	3.50	−2.64	.01***
Special education G40	−23.15	4.25	−5.45	.00***
Scaled reading pretest (grand centered) G50	0.55	0.03	15.68	.00***
Scaled math pretest (grand centered) G60	0.20	0.03	6.18	.00***
Impute reading G70	−1.13	3.55	−0.32	.75
Impute ELD G80	−2.95	2.44	−1.21	.23
Beginning ELD G90	−8.03	3.86	−2.08	.04**
English proficient G100	5.08	2.70	1.88	.06*
Parent no high school G110	−1.47	2.05	−0.72	.47
Missing parent education G120	−2.78	2.93	−0.95	0.34
Grade 3	−3.18	4.40	−0.72	0.47
Grade 4	−3.73	4.90	−0.76	0.45
Grade 5	−9.54	6.28	−1.52	0.13

Note. Reliability of β_0 = .72. Variance components: τ_{00} = 53.74; σ^2 = 362.03. G refers to γ. Proportion of between-class variation explained by reading TES = .34. Scale is a 1-point gain in reading on the spring 2001 test. TES = teacher evaluation scores; ELD = English language development.

*p < .10. **p < .05. ***p < .001.

resented in the random intercept model was explained by the TES. Table 8 reports the coefficient, standard error, and *t* ratio and proportion of variance explained for each subject. This analysis confirmed findings from the correlation analysis that the literacy TES was the best predictor of variation in classroom effects, explaining 34% of the variation. Similar models were run for mathematics, language arts, and the composite measure. Results of those models are in Table 8.

The composite TES was likewise statistically significant, explaining 13% of the variation in student outcomes. As in the correlation analysis, TES in mathematics and language arts were not statistically significant predictors of classroom effects. Prior research has shown the importance of alignment between enacted and tested curriculum in predicting teacher effects on student performance on achievement tests (Porter & Smithson, 2000a). The lack of relationship between TES and classroom effects in language arts is potentially attributable to a lack of alignment between the Vaughn teacher rubrics (which emphasize ELD, including oral language) and the SAT–9 language arts test (which emphasizes grammar and organization of writ-

Table 8

Teacher Evaluation Scores as Level 2 Predictors Across Subjects

Variable	Reading	Mathematics	Language Arts	Composite
Coefficient (scale = 1-point gain on spring 2001 test)	14.18	7.22	6.30	10.07
SE	3.81	5.63	4.29	4.59
t ratio	3.71**	1.28	1.47	2.19*
Proportion of explained classroom-level variance	.34	.03	.01	.13

*$p < .05$. **$p < .001$.

ing). The lack of relationship in mathematics was explored through the qualitative portion of the study.

The final question explored in the quantitative analysis was whether teacher characteristics of certification and years of experience (on which both the traditional salary structure and much research on teacher effects are based) were significant predictors of variation in classroom effects at Vaughn. This issue was examined using models identical to those used to test TES except that teacher characteristics were inserted at Level 2 instead of TES. Full results are presented in Gallagher (2002). Across all of the subject areas, none of these variables (full certification, bilingual certification, being a salary Category 2 or 3 teacher, less than 2 years experience, 5 years or more experience, and greater than 5 years experience) was statistically significant. Given the small sample size and the design of the pay system (which may provide an advantage to Vaughn in recruiting temporarily certified teachers of higher than average quality), this result should not be interpreted to mean that these factors are not potentially important indicators of teacher quality. However, the lack of statistical significance for these predictors can be compared to the TES scores utilized in similar (the only difference being the predictor itself) models with the same sample; the TES predicted more of the existing variation, especially in literacy. This supports prior research (e.g., Hanushek, 1971) that has raised the issue of the need to improve the nature of teacher characteristics recorded to include variables more proximal to instruction.

Looking across these analyses, it is possible to draw several conclusions:

- Results confirm findings from other studies in that there was significant variation in student achievement that can be attributed to the classroom level—classroom effects.

- Overall, the Vaughn teacher evaluation system had a statistically significant relationship to classroom effects, that is, value-added learning growth. The strength of the relationship in literacy was much stronger than would have been anticipated from previous research.
- Traditional teacher quality variables (e.g., licensure, experience) appeared to be insignificant predictors of variation in student achievement, especially when compared to some more proximal indicators of instruction such as the literacy evaluation score.
- The results from both the correlation analysis and the insertion of TES into Level 2 of the model showed a striking contrast between reading and the other subject area variables.

The last of those findings offered the potential to be highly instructive in terms of developing theory about what factors can lead to a more or less valid teacher evaluation system. As a result, in the second part of the study, I compared the evaluation system in literacy and mathematics and dropped the language arts due to lack of alignment between the evaluation system and measures of student outcomes.

Summary of the Results of the Qualitative Component

The first step of the qualitative component of the study was to analyze the Vaughn teaching rubrics, California state standards for students, descriptions of adopted curricular materials, and professional development records for the past 3 years in both reading and mathematics. (Although it was also desirable to analyze the augmented California version of the SAT–9, no analysis was possible because it was a secure form of the test and Harcourt Brace was not willing to release the necessary information for this study.) These analyses led to several important findings:

- The Vaughn teacher rubrics focused on teaching decoding, comprehension, and more complex analysis in literacy. In mathematics, the focus was largely on procedures and routine problem solving instead of mathematical reasoning.
- Vaughn has invested heavily in professional development in literacy (61 hr in which 100% of faculty participated during the 2000–01 school year) including participation in the state's RESULTS program, which provides teachers with specific diagnostic information about students' reading skills and suggests strategies to help students achieve standards. In mathematics, only the publishers of adopted math series have provided formal professional development. As a result, although Vaughn teachers

have had similar and extensive school-based professional development in reading, teachers' exposure to professional development in mathematics was partially dependent on the length of employment at Vaughn.

• Vaughn has had a stable and highly coordinated reading curriculum over the past few years. The adoption of RESULTS provides teachers with information about which skills their students need to improve to meet standards. The mathematics curriculum, in contrast, has vacillated from a conceptual/manipulatives to a basic skills/drill philosophy for the past few years. The adoption of a new math series aligned with standards during the 2001–02 school year created significant frustration for teachers who were not comfortable with its emphasis on algebra and mathematical reasoning in elementary grades.

• Vaughn has a daily literacy instruction block of over 2 hr. This time ensures at least relative parity across classes in the amount of instruction devoted to reading. Symbolically, it also shows that literacy is considered to be the most important subject.

• Although the Vaughn teaching rubrics were closely aligned with the student standards in reading, the mathematics teaching rubrics focused mainly on a subset of the standards—basic procedural skills.

Taken as a whole, these findings suggest that the Vaughn staff probably has a relatively unified vision of effective teaching in literacy that is well aligned with the state standards for student learning. In math, the teacher rubrics and history of changes in adopted materials suggest that the vision of effective teaching potentially varied more across teachers and was less aligned with the state standards for mathematics instruction.

Interviews with teachers and evaluators corroborated the findings from the document analyses. In reading, teachers relied heavily on RESULTS to understand students' needs and plan instruction. All teachers used a variety of strategies to address both basic skills and more complex reading goals. Both teachers and evaluators consistently spoke of the importance of building students higher order thinking skills in literacy. Evaluators had deep pedagogical content knowledge of literacy instruction, with two of three stating that their own skills were stronger in literacy than in math.

There were some differences across teachers in the sample that seemed to influence their evaluation scores and classroom effects. One interesting trend was that teachers with the broadest literacy goals, who spoke the most about student enjoyment of reading and the broader social purposes of reading, tended to get higher TES and lower classroom effects than would be predicted. This result suggests two things: First, the broader goals may have reduced the alignment between the enacted and tested curriculum; second, evaluators appeared to have a bias toward a teaching style (which they described as "whole language") that not only utilizes a broad range of instructional strategies but also focuses on goals beyond skill (both basic and higher order) development. In contrast, one teacher who had skills-oriented goals and reported paying attention to the SAT–9 had higher classroom effects than would have been predicted from her evaluation score.[3]

The final interesting finding was that teachers had a generally high sense of efficacy in literacy instruction. One teacher did not; as could be expected from previous research, her classroom effects were lower than would have been predicted from her evaluation scores.

Interviews with both teachers and evaluators painted a picture of mathematics instruction at Vaughn that was quite different from literacy instruction. In contrast to the focus on higher order thinking skills in literacy, Vaughn's vision of effective instruction in mathematics was oriented largely toward solving routine computation and word problems. Within this subset of skills required by the student standards, Vaughn teachers and evaluators had a range of strategies for facilitating student success; however the relatively narrow range of evaluators' knowledge of mathematics instruction (focused on basic skills) appeared to have limited their ability to distinguish amongst variations in teacher quality in mathematics.

The most illustrative example of the overall lack of alignment between Vaughn mathematics instruction, evaluation, and student standards came from a teacher (who had high classroom effects and average teacher evaluation scores) who was providing instruction focused on building students' mathematical reasoning skills through a math journal. Although the usefulness of this strategy has been discussed in literature on reform mathematics instruction (e.g., see Lampert, 2001; National Council of Teachers of Mathematics, 2000), the teacher was criticized by her evaluator for teaching writing during a math lesson. This comment provided evidence that both typical instruction and teacher evaluation in mathematics was not well aligned with the state standards.

Teachers also appeared to have had a lower sense of efficacy in mathematics instruction compared to literacy instruction. Teachers routinely discussed how their students' limited English vocabulary hindered their progress in mathematics. It is interesting that teachers in the literacy sample did not discuss how this limited student performance in reading in which lack of English fluency could be a greater learning inhibitor; instead, they discussed their strategies for building students' English vocabulary. This finding corroborates the finding of other research (Tschannen-Moran et al., 1998) that efficacy can be subject—as well as context—specific.

---

[3]Of the 12 interviewed teachers, 2 were male. To protect the anonymity of the male participants, all teachers are referred to as "she" in this article.

The qualitative part of the study suggested that the less significant relationship between TES and classroom effects in mathematics was caused by low alignment between California's mathematics standards and Vaughn math teaching and teacher evaluation. The three greatest sources of the lower alignment appear to have been

- Lack of teacher knowledge and comfort with some areas of the state mathematics standards, particularly mathematical reasoning and algebra.
- Lack of evaluator understanding of the importance of and strategies for building students' higher order thinking skills in mathematics.
- Vaughn's teaching rubrics, which articulated a vision of effective mathematics teaching that focused on a subset of state mathematics standards, namely mathematical procedures and solving routine math problems.

The lower alignment between state standards and Vaughn's instruction and teacher evaluation led to TES scores that were not significant predictors of variations in classroom effects in mathematics.

The qualitative stage of the study thus provided some possible explanations for why the relationship between TES and classroom effects was stronger in literacy than in mathematics. For several reasons, Vaughn teachers and evaluators were more knowledgeable about California's intended curriculum in literacy than they were in math. Teachers were cognizant of a broad range of state goals for literacy instruction and had a variety of strategies for helping students achieve them. Their use of ongoing student assessment to plan instruction and utilization of a variety of instructional materials demonstrated that, as a whole, teachers had a relatively high level of pedagogical content knowledge in reading. Evaluators were similarly knowledgeable about reading instruction and thus gave more effective teachers higher ratings. In contrast, the lesser degree of pedagogical content knowledge for Vaughn teachers and evaluators in math led to curriculum and instruction that was not highly aligned to state standards and evaluation that appeared less able to distinguish among various teachers' skills in mathematics instruction. Across subjects, both lower alignment between intended and enacted curriculum and lower efficacy appeared to weaken the relationship between individual teachers' evaluation scores and classroom effects.

Implications

Prior to discussing the implications of the findings, it is important to take a step back to understand the policy context in which Vaughn exists, which offers one potential explanation for Vaughn's emphasis on literacy over mathematics instruction. In 1998, California voters passed Proposition 227, which mandated English as the language of public school instruction and required all students who have been enrolled in publicly funded schools for over 1 year to take standardized tests in English. In addition, the state has several accountability policies that reward schools based on student performance on the English SAT–9. Because most of Vaughn's students are English language learners, it behooves Vaughn to put substantial energy into ensuring that teachers have the capacity to help students succeed on standardized tests in English. Furthermore, Vaughn students scored higher on standardized tests in mathematics (52nd percentile) than reading (29th percentile) or language arts (35th percentile), which was not surprising, because mathematics performance would likely be less inhibited by lack of full English fluency than performance in reading or language arts. Although the findings of this study could be interpreted as critical of Vaughn's lower levels of professional development and pedagogical content knowledge in mathematics, from a broader perspective, Vaughn's focus on literacy can be seen as a highly rational choice given the state policy context.

It is also important to note that although the correlation between TES and classroom effects in mathematics was not statistically significant, it was only slightly below the mean correlation reported in Heneman's (1986) meta-analysis of the relationship between supervisory ratings and employee outcomes (.23 in mathematics at Vaughn compared to .27 overall found in Heneman's meta-analysis). This finding suggests that although the Vaughn teacher evaluation system clearly has room for improvement in mathematics, the strength of the relationship between evaluation scores and classroom effects in literacy is more remarkable.

Seen from this perspective, this study makes an important contribution to research and practice by providing an understanding of how teacher evaluation can be dramatically improved. Furthermore, the qualitative component of the study suggests that using subject-specific evaluations conducted by evaluators who have expertise (pedagogical content knowledge) in instruction of the subject they are evaluating can improve the validity of teacher evaluation systems.

Additional research would be useful to see if the contrast between the strength of the relationship in literacy and mathematics remains the same as Vaughn undertakes planned professional development in mathematics. This research could add valuable knowledge about the importance of subject-specific conceptions of teacher quality and the usefulness of subject-specific evaluation. This has enormous practical implications, especially for high schools where content specialists are typically evaluated by principals who rarely share teachers' content specialization.

Finally, the unexpectedly strong relationship between TES and classroom effects in literacy at Vaughn suggests the need for replication and expansion of this research. Although the findings of this study are interesting, they need to be tested both over time and in other sites to provide for broader generalization of theory about factors that affect the validity of teacher evaluation systems. As schools attempt to educate students to challenging academic standards, improvements in teacher evaluation could play a critical role in identifying areas in which teachers need to improve their skills. The importance of validity also increases when the stakes attached to evaluations get higher as is the case with knowledge- and skills-based pay. Thus, it is important that this study be replicated in other sites to develop an expanded knowledge base about increasing the validity of teacher evaluation systems.

References

Ashton, P. T., & Webb, R. B. (1986). *Making a difference: Teachers' sense of efficacy and student achievement.* New York: Longman.

Bransford, J. D., Brown, A. L., & Cocking, R. R. (Eds.). (1999). *How people learn: Brain, mind, experience, and school.* Washington, DC: National Academy Press.

Bryk, A. S., & Raudenbush, S. W. (1992). *Hierarchical linear models.* Newbury Park, CA: Sage.

Coleman, J. S. (1990). *Equality and achievement in education.* Boulder, CO: Westview.

Corcoran, T. B. (1995). *Helping teachers teach well: Transforming professional development* (CPRE Policy Brief No. RB–16). Philadelphia: Consortium for Policy Research in Education.

Danielson, C. (1996). *Enhancing professional practice: A framework for teaching.* Alexandria, VA: Association for Supervision and Curriculum Development.

Darling-Hammond, L. (1999, January–February). America's future: Educating teachers. *Academe, 85,* 26–33.

Darling-Hammond, L. (2000). Teacher quality and student achievement: A review of state policy evidence. *Education Policy Analysis Archives, 8*(1), 50.

Darling-Hammond, L., & McLaughlin, M. (1995, April). Policies that support professional teacher development in an era of reform. *Phi Delta Kappan, 76,* 642–644.

Dembo, M. H., & Gibson, S. (1985). Teachers' sense of efficacy: An important factor in school improvement. *The Elementary School Journal, 86,* 174–185.

Du, Y., & Heistad, D. (1999, April). *School performance accountability in Minneapolis public schools.* Paper presented at the American Educational Research Association, Montreal, Canada.

Entwisle, D. R., Alexander, K. L., & Olson, L. S. (1997). *Children, schools, and inequality.* Boulder, CO: Westview.

Gallagher, H. A. (2002). *The relationship between measures of teacher quality and student achievement: The case of Vaughn Elementary.* Unpublished doctoral dissertation, University of Wisconsin–Madison.

Grossman, P. L. (1990). *The making of a teacher: Teacher knowledge and teacher education.* New York: Teachers College Press.

Hanushek, E. (1971). Teacher characteristics and gains in student achievement: Estimation using micro data. *The American Economic Review, 61,* 280–288.

Hanushek, E. A., Kain, J. F., & Rivkin, S. G. (1998). *Teachers, schools, and academic achievement.* Cambridge, MA: National Bureau of Economic Research.

Haycock, K. (1998). Good teaching matters: How well-qualified teachers can close the gap. *Thinking K–16, 3*(2), 1–14.

Heistad, D. (1999, April). *Teachers who beat the odds: Value-added reading instruction in Minneapolis 2nd grade classrooms.* Paper presented at the American Educational Research Association Conference, Montreal, Canada.

Heneman, R. L. (1986). The relationship between supervisory ratings and results-oriented measures of performance: A meta-analysis. *Personnel Psychology, 39,* 811–826.

Kellor, E., Milanowski, T., Odden, A., & Gallagher, H. A. (2001). *How Vaughn next century learning center developed a knowledge- and skill-pay program.* Consortium for Policy Research in Education, Wisconsin Center for Education Research, University of Wisconsin–Madison. Retrieved from http://www.wcer.wisc.edu/cpre/papers/pdf/vaughn%20KSBP% 208-01.pdf

Lampert, M. (2001). *Teaching problems and the problems of teaching.* New Haven, CT: Yale University Press.

Lumpe, A. T., Haney, J. J., & Czerniak, C. M. (2000). Assessing teachers' beliefs about their science teaching context. *Journal of Research in Science Teaching, 37,* 275–292.

National Council of Teachers of Mathematics. (2000). *Principles and standards for school mathematics.* Reston, VA: Author.

Medley, D. M., & Coker, H. (1987). The accuracy of principals' judgments of teacher performance. *The Journal of Educational Research, 80,* 242–247.

Mendro, R. L. (1998). Student achievement and school and teacher accountability. *Journal of Personnel Evaluation in Education, 12,* 257–267.

Meyer, R. H. (1996a). Comments on chapters two, three, and four. In H. F. Ladd (Ed.), *Holding schools accountable: Performance-based reform in education* (pp. 137–145). Washington, DC: Brookings Institute.

Meyer, R. H. (1996b). Value-added indicators of school performance. In E. A. Hanushek & D. W. Jorgenson (Eds.), *Improving America's schools: The role of incentives* (pp. 197–123). Washington, DC: National Academy Press.

Meyer, R. H. (1997). Value-added indicators of school performance: A primer. *Economics of Education Review, 16,* 283–301.

Milanowski, A., & Gallagher, H. A. (2001). *Vaughn next century learning center performance pay survey school report.* Consortium for Policy Research in Education, Wisconsin Center for Education Research, University of Wisconsin–Madison.

Odden, A., & Kelley, C. (2002). *Paying teachers for what they know and do: New and smarter compensation strategies to improve schools* (2nd ed.). Thousand Oaks, CA: Corwin Press.

Peterson, K. D. (2000). *Teacher evaluation: A comprehensive guide to new directions and practices* (2nd ed.). Thousand Oaks, CA: Corwin Press.

Porter, A. C., & Smithson, J. L. (2000a, April). *Alignment of state testing programs, NAEP and reports of teacher practice in mathematics and science in grades 4 and 8.* Paper presented at the American Educational Research Association, New Orleans, LA.

Porter, A. C., & Smithson, J. L. (2000b). *Are content standards being implemented in the classroom? A methodology and some tentative answers.* Unpublished manuscript.

Porter, A. C., Youngs, P., & Odden, A. (2001). Advances in teacher assessments and their uses. In V. Richardson (Ed.), *Handbook of research on teaching* (4th ed., pp. 259–297). Washington, DC: American Educational Research Education.

Ross, J. (1998). The antecedents and consequences of teacher efficacy. In J. Brophy (Ed.), *Advances in research on teaching* (Vol. 7, pp. 49–74). Greenwich, CT: JAI.

Rowan, B. (1999). *Assessing teacher quality: insights from school effectiveness research.* School of Education, University of Michigan, Ann Arbor.

Rowan, B. (2001). *What large-scale, survey research tells us about teacher effects on student achievement: Insights from the prospects study of elementary schools.* Ann Arbor, MI: Consortium for Policy Research in Education.

Shulman, L. S. (1987). Knowledge and teaching: Foundation of the new reform. *Harvard Educational Review, 57,* 1–22.

Snijders, T., & Bosker, R. (1999). *Multilevel analysis: An introduction to basic and advanced multilevel modeling.* London: Sage Hill.

Soodak, L. C., & Podell, D. M. (1998). Teacher efficacy and the vulnerability of the difficult-to-teach student. *Advances in Research on Teaching, 7,* 75–109.

Tschannen-Moran, M., Hoy, A. W., & Hoy, W. K. (1998). Teacher efficacy: Its meaning and measure. *Review of Educational Research, 68,* 202–248.

Webster, W. J., & Mendro, R. L. (1997). The Dallas value-added accountability system. In J. Millman (Ed.), *Grading teachers, grading schools: Is student achievement a valid evaluation measure?* (pp. 81–99). Thousand Oaks, CA: Corwin Press.

WestEd. (1998). *Case study: Vaughn next century learning center.* Los Angeles: WestEd, Los Angeles Unified School District.

Wright, S. P., Horn, S. P., & Sanders, W. L. (1997). Teacher and classroom context effects on student achievement: Implications for teacher evaluation. *Journal of Personnel Evaluation in Education, 11,* 57–67.

PEABODY JOURNAL OF EDUCATION, 79(4), 108–125

Alignment of Human Resource Practices and Teacher Performance Competency

Herbert G. Heneman III
Consortium for Policy Research in Education
and Graduate School of Business
University of Wisconsin–Madison

Anthony T. Milanowski
Consortium for Policy Research in Education
University of Wisconsin–Madison

In this article, we argue that human resource (HR) management practices are important components of strategies for improving student achievement in

An earlier version of this article was presented at the 2003 annual meeting of the American Educational Research Association, Chicago on April 21. The research reported in this article was supported in part by a grant from the U.S. Department of Education, Office of Educational Research and Improvement, National Institute on Educational Governance, Finance, Policymaking, and Management to the Consortium for Policy Research in Education (CPRE) and the Wisconsin Center for Educational Research, School of Education, University of Wisconsin–Madison (Grant OERI–R3086A60003). The opinions expressed are those of the authors and do not necessarily reflect the view of the National Institute on Educational Governance, Finance, Policymaking, and Management, Office of Educational Research and Improvement, U.S. Department of Education; the institutional partners of CPRE; or the Wisconsin Center for Education Research.

For their generous assistance in providing information and feedback, we thank Susan Raudabaugh of the Cincinnati School District and Sharyn Appolloni, Laura Dancer, and Lynn Sawyer of the Washoe County School District.

Requests for reprints should be sent to Herbert G. Heneman III, University of Wisconsin–Madison, Consortium for Policy Research in Education, 1025 West Johnson Street, Madison, WI 53706. E-mail: hheneman@bus.wisc.edu an accountability environment. We present a framework illustrating the alignment of educational HR management practices to a teacher performance competency model, which in turn is aligned with student achievement goals. We identify and illustrate the various HR practices that could be aligned to the performance competency model and to each other. These HR practices include recruitment, selection, induction, mentoring, professional development, compensation, performance management, and instructional leadership. We then describe HR practices in 2 districts where empirical links between teacher competency and student achievement were shown (Cincinnati and Washoe County) and evaluate how much alignment was in place. We discuss the importance of HR alignment analysis for diagnosing districts' teacher quality improvement efforts, and we present suggestions for future research on the strategic use of HR management in K–12 educational organizations.

Many school districts are feeling pressures for improved organizational performance, first from state testing and accountability systems and more recently from the "adequate yearly progress" requirements of the federal No Child Left Behind Act of 2001. Both state accountability systems and the federal act, for better or worse, define organizational performance largely in terms of improvements in student achievement on tests. Among the important influences on student achievement are teachers' instructional practices. Recent research (e.g., Darling-Hammond & Youngs, 2002; Mendro, 1998; Rowan, Correnti, & Miller, 2002; Wright, Horn, & Sanders, 1997) and policy making (e.g., the No Child Left Behind Act requirement that there be a "highly qualified" teacher in every classroom by 2005–06) have emphasized the importance of teachers and teaching practice as an input to student achievement. Therefore, a logical strategy for districts seeking to improve student achievement, as defined by these accountability systems, is to improve teacher quality.

Most policymakers are immediately drawn to making changes in the instructional program to improve teaching: curriculum, time scheduling, pedagogical techniques, and so forth. Yet they often overlook the need to support these changes by changing district human resource (HR) management practices. HR management practices collectively are the means for acquiring, developing, and retaining a high-quality workforce, one that can carry out the instructional programs thought to lead to improved student achievement.

In the private sector, research has shown that there are clear links between the nature and quality of HR management practices and various indicators of organizational performance (e.g., Batt, 2002; Becker & Huselid, 1998; Gratton & Truss, 2003; Wright, Dunford, & Snell, 2001). It is thought that HR management practices affect organizational performance through employee performance competencies. That is, choices among HR management practices lead to differences in the effectiveness of the workforce in contributing to organizational performance. This research has encouraged interest in the development of performance competency models, which define the abilities, skills, and behaviors thought to contribute to organizational performance and which guide the design and implementation of HR management activities (Heneman & Judge, 2003; Schippman, 1999).

Building an HR management system to support the teacher performance competencies that define teacher quality requires developing or adapting a model that specifies these competencies. Performance competencies are actual behaviors engaged in by teachers that theory and research has suggested are linked to student achievement. Performance competencies thus differentiate between more and less effective teachers. The Framework for Teaching developed by Danielson (1996) and used as the foundation for teacher evaluation systems by the Cincinnati and Washoe County school districts is an example of a performance competency model. According to Danielson (1996), its four domains (Planning and Preparation, The Classroom Environment, Instruction, and Professional Responsibilities) and 22 components constitute a behavioral mapping of "those aspects of a teacher's responsibilities that have been documented through empirical studies and theoretical research as promoting improved student learning" (p. 1). It is, of course, central to a strategy of improving performance competency to improve student achievement that the performance competencies be related to student achievement. The articles by Gallagher (2004/this issue), Milanowski (2004/this issue), and Kimball, White, Milanowski, and Borman (2004/this issue) provide support for the potential usefulness of the Framework competency model as the foundation for a teacher HR management system by showing an empirical link between teachers' rated performance on Framework-based assessment instruments and value-added measures of student achievement.

In this article, we extend the HR management practices/performance competency/organizational effectiveness paradigm to school systems. First, we describe an HR alignment model that identifies and illustrates the various HR practices that could be aligned to the performance competency model and to each other. We describe the actual HR practices in two of the three districts where empirical links between measure teacher competency and student achievement were shown (Cincinnati and Washoe County) and evaluate how much alignment was in place. We then discuss the importance of HR alignment analysis for diagnosing districts' teacher quality improvement efforts. We conclude by suggesting several caveats and suggestions for future research.

HR Alignment Model

Construction of an HR alignment model must be preceded by several things. The beginning point for any HR alignment model is to identify the focal point for alignment. That focal point is the overriding educational objective chosen by or specified for the school district. In the model described next, the focal objective is improved student achievement, an important objective for most school districts. Imbedded within this objective is the assumption that the district knows the learning areas (math, science, language arts, etc.) in which improved student achievement is sought and that the district has chosen student achievement measures for obtaining assessments in those learning areas.

A second requirement for an HR alignment model is specification of a teacher performance competency model that captures the essence of the teacher role—the general desired teacher behaviors and behavioral standards, which in turn are theory and research based. The Framework for Teaching is an example of such a teacher performance competency model. The teacher competencies contained in the model are considered key causal determinants or drivers of student achievement. Moreover, ideally, there is supportive empirical research demonstrating performance competency/student achievement links. As noted, there is such evidence for the Framework for Teaching.

A third factor to address in construction of an HR alignment model is the set of HR practices for which alignment is sought. In this example, HR practices were identified in eight HR functional areas: recruitment, selection, induction, mentoring, professional development, compensation, performance management, and instructional leaders. These eight areas cover most of the HR domain in most districts for which alignment is appropriate. That is, each area has certain practices that could be undertaken to influence teacher competency. Excluded are HR support areas such as payroll and technology, which by themselves are not performance competency focused. Within each of the eight functional areas, components must be specified to capture specific HR practices. Table 1 provides the eight functional areas and components for each along with descriptions of them. These guided HR alignment data collection in the two districts.

Based on the preceding considerations, the actual HR alignment model was constructed. It is shown in Figure 1. At the top of the model are the actual student achievement goals of the district, which serve as the ultimate strategic objectives for the district. Feeding into, and driving, student achievement is teacher performance competency. In this study, teacher performance competency was represented by the Framework for Teaching (Danielson, 1996) as adapted by each of the two school districts. In turn,

Table 1

Specific HR Practices in the HR Alignment Model

HR Areas	Definition
1. Recruitment	
Applicant pools	Sources of applicants based on the knowledge, skills, and abilities necessary for performance competency vis-à-vis the *competency* model
Information	Information provided to applicants about the teacher performance competency model and the HR practices aligned to it
2. Selection	
Licensure	Licensing requirements and the basis for them
Assessments	Methods of assessing likely teacher performance competency
Standards	Actual hiring requirements and "cut scores" for accepting applicants
3. Induction	
Preservice	Assistance and information provided to teachers prior to start of school
On-the-job	Assistance and information provided to teachers on the job as relates to performance expectations and the performance competency model
4. Mentoring	
Content	Subject areas, pedagogy, social support, school and classroom procedures
Participants	Who provides the mentoring (e.g., formal mentor, other teachers)
5. Professional development	
Content	Subject areas, activities (e.g., courses, inservice projects)
Teacher planning	Mechanisms for focusing and assisting teachers' choices of professional development content

6. Compensation	
Base pay	Regular salary for teaching duties during contract period
Variable pay	Supplements on top of base pay for additional duties or performance (e.g., bonuses); base pay increases linked to performance
Hiring packages	Regular salary plus other financial inducements, such as hiring bonus, loan forgiveness, tuition reimbursement, housing assistance, or regular salary "bump" for high quality
7. Performance management	
Teacher evaluation	System for appraising teacher's performance
Feedback/Coaching	Information given to teacher about results of the appraisal; assistance to teacher in how to maintain and improve performance
Goal setting	Formal setting of specific goals, with timetables, to guide performance planning and improvement
Remediation	Activities for intervention and assistance to low-performing teachers; outplacement and termination
8. Instructional leaders	
Selection	Assessing and choosing leaders based on their previous teacher evaluations and/or how well they conduct teacher evaluations of the performance of their teachers
Training	Knowledge and skill building given in how to conduct and improve teacher evaluation and performance management
Performance management	Appraisal, feedback, coaching, goal setting, performance planning, discipline, termination

Note. HR = human resources.

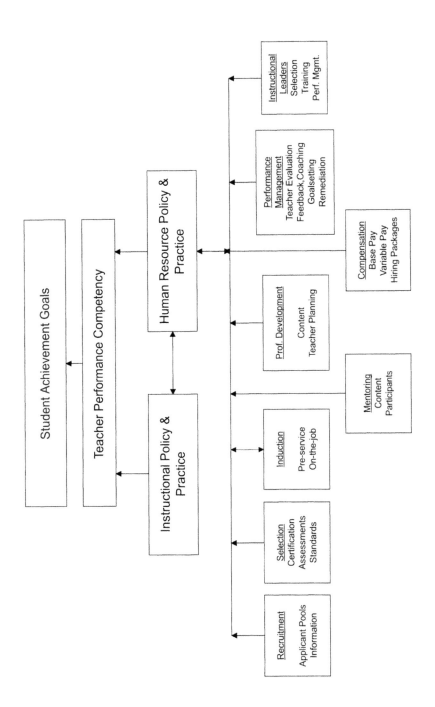

Figure 1. Model of human resource management systems alignment.

teacher performance competency was the result of a combination of instructional and HR practices. Finally, the eight functional areas of HR practice and key components of each are shown.

Imbedded within the HR alignment model are two types of alignment—vertical and horizontal. Vertical alignment represents the degree of linkage between a particular HR functional practice and teacher performance competency. Consider, for example, HR selection. It has three specific components that must be aligned to teacher performance competency—certification, assessment, and hiring standards. To create vertical alignment, licensing requirements should ensure some degree of minimal proficiency in the teacher performance competencies (e.g., completion of Praxis I and II), assessment of applicants should focus on their likelihood of successful on-the-job performance in the competency areas (e.g., through a structured behavioral interview or a work sample), and hiring standards should be set at high levels so that only the best quality applicants are hired. Horizontal alignment represents the linkages among the HR practices such that the practices are internally consistent and reinforcing. In selection, for example, the use of high hiring standards might be linked to the compensation area by providing the favorable starting salaries and hiring packages (e.g., signing bonuses, relocation assistance) necessary to attract the high-quality applicants. HR practices must also be linked horizontally to instructional practices. In selection of job applicants, for example, the content of a work sample assessment should reflect the particular types of instructional practices desired by the district.

In summary, we posit that teacher quality or performance competency (such as represented by the Framework for Teaching) is a primary driver of student achievement and that teacher competency is a joint product of instructional and HR practices. Historically, HR practices have received relatively little attention as potentially important drivers of teacher performance competency improvement. To function as such drivers, HR practices must be vertically aligned to a valid teacher performance competency model, and HR practices must also be aligned horizontally to instructional practices and to each other.

We next describe case studies of HR alignment in two districts that have adopted the Framework for Teaching as a performance competency model that formed the basis for the new teacher evaluation systems. The various HR practices then began to be aligned to the evaluation system itself and to each other.

Method

Data for the study were gathered from the Cincinnati and Washoe County school districts. The HR alignment model (Figure 1) served to identify and focus the specific HR practices data collected. Data came from interviews (with HR staff and other administrators), archival documents (policies, brochures, handbooks), and district Web sites (the employment/ career section). For each of the eight functional HR areas and their specific components, examples of HR practices that illustrated aligned HR practices were sought as was done by Gratton and Truss (2003). Given the exploratory nature of the study, we did not have a predetermined checklist of practices sought. Rather, we simply sought descriptions of all HR practices, and from these, we discovered which ones illustrated examples of HR practice alignment. For such practice, a brief synopsis of it was entered into Table 2 (Cincinnati) or Table 3 (Washoe County). If no example was found, this was also noted in the tables. The result is an identification and brief synopsis of all of the aligned HR practices we were able to uncover in each district in the eight functional HR areas.

Results

Table 2 shows the aligned HR practices in the Cincinnati school district. Within each of the eight HR areas, there are some examples of HR practice alignment, although examples for some components within each area are lacking. Particular attention to alignment by the district appears for recruitment, selection, orientation, mentoring, and two components of performance management (the teacher evaluation system and remediation). There is some alignment for professional development and compensation, although much of the proposed compensation system was rejected by a vote of the teachers and is subject to renegotiation by the teachers association. Currently, a provision remains that limits movement to the final two steps in the salary schedule to those who attain satisfactory scores on the evaluation. Alignment is almost totally lacking for instructional leaders (principals and assistant principals), no doubt a reflection of the attention given to teachers as opposed to administrators during design and implementation of the new teacher evaluation system and other aligned HR practices.

Table 3 displays the HR alignment for Washoe County. Examples of alignment are present for each of the eight HR practice areas, although several components of those areas lack any examples. Most alignment appears for orientation, mentoring, professional development, and performance management. There is less alignment for instructional leadership and very little alignment for recruitment, selection, and compensation. HR alignment practices in Washoe County thus vary in type and areas of emphasis relative to Cincinnati.

Table 2

Examples of HR Alignment: Cincinnati School District

HR Practices	Examples of Alignment
1. Recruitment	
Applicant pools	New teachers are recruited from universities (e.g., University of Cincinnati) where students receive experience with, and exposure to, the Framework for Teaching and the Teacher Evaluation System via class work and internships
Information	The teacher evaluation system is prominently displayed and described on the Cincinnati Public Schools Web site, next to the online employment application
2. Selection	
Certification	Labor contract specifies all new teachers must (a) hold a provisional license, (b) successfully complete the Entry Year Program about the Framework for Teaching, (c) receive their initial evaluation under the teacher evaluation system within the first 2 years, and (d) not be required to teach outside their areas of certification/licensure
Assessment	A staffing specialist in the HR Department uses a structured behavioral interview to assess the applicant's competence in each of the four domains the teacher evaluation system
Hiring standards	Job offer preference is given to applicants with advanced degrees in the subject area in which they plan to teach. Applicants who do well in the behavioral interview are offered a job immediately; other applicants must go through additional assessments
3. Induction	
Preservice	Prior to the new school year, new hires are given information about the teacher evaluation system as part of a 2½-day orientation program
On-the-job	Labor contract specifies that before teachers are evaluated they must receive an orientation to the teacher evaluation system and that special assistance regarding the teacher evaluation system will be given to new teachers using resources provided by the principal, consulting teacher, and others. Meetings with the principal about the teacher evaluation system are common. The Entry Year Program for new teachers is based on the Pathwise program of the Educational Testing Service, which provides exposure to the four teaching domains and accompanying standards

(continued)

Table 2 *(Continued)*

HR Practices	Examples of Alignment
4. Mentoring	
Content	There is a formal Peer Assistance and Evaluation program in which new teachers are assigned to a CT. The CT provides orientation assistance with the curriculum and content issues, group seminars on selected topics, and guidance on the four domains (especially the Classroom Management domain) of the teacher evaluation system. The CT conducts the new teacher's first evaluation and assists in an intervention program for new teachers who receive low scores
Participation	New teachers and CTs participate. Under the five-step career progression system, the CTs are at the advanced or accomplished teacher steps (the top two steps) and are in the same subject area and grade level as the new teacher
5. Professional development	
Content	There are voluntary introductory courses about the teacher evaluation system taught in the district's separate Mayerson Teaching Academy and voluntary study groups that use Pathwise to focus on inquires about the teaching standards in the Framework for Teaching
Teacher planning	By state law, a teacher wishing to fulfill license renewal requirements must design an individual professional development plan. The plan must be based on goals derived from the teaching standards in the teacher evaluation system. The plan can go beyond traditional coursework and workshops to other job-related activities. The plan must be approved by the legally required local Professional Development Committee
6. Compensation	
Base pay	The proposed Teacher Quality Program establishes five career levels (apprentice, novice, career, advanced, and accomplished) and a separate base pay for each level; pay progression within each level is based on seniority, with up to four steps for each level
Variable pay	The Teacher Quality Program was to provide for movement between the five career levels based on teacher evaluation system scores. Also, teachers at the top two career levels are eligible to be chosen as lead teachers, with a base pay increment of up to $5,500. The Teacher Quality Program proposal was rejected by a vote of the Teacher Association membership and is now in the process of renegotiation
Hiring packages	No examples available

7. Performance management

Teacher evaluation Teacher evaluation is derived from the Framework for Teaching. The teachers are evaluated in up to all four domains (planning and preparing for student learning, creating an environment for learning, teaching for learning, and professionalism), which contain a set of 17 performance standards. For each standard, there is a 4-point rating scale depicting four levels of performance using behavioral descriptors (rubrics) to help the evaluator make rating judgments. Judgments are made on the basis of multiple source of evidence. Evaluators have received training in the teacher evaluation system

Feedback/Coaching The evaluator must provide written feedback to the teacher about the ratings, using standards language couched in the teacher evaluation system

Goal setting No examples available

Remediation An intervention is conducted by a consulting teacher for a teacher who received unacceptable ratings on the teacher evaluation system. The intervention consists of discussion, performance improvement planning, and mentoring by the consulting teacher, using the teacher evaluation system standards. The teacher's principal may also recommend intervention to a teacher association management committee

8. Instructional leaders

Selection Leader teachers perform various roles, such as curriculum specialist, assessor, consultant, schoolwide leader teacher, subject area leader, and instructional team leader. To be selected, at a minimum, they must be at the advanced or accomplished teacher level in the Teacher Quality Program
There are no examples for principals and assistant principals.

Training Administrators (most often, principals and assistance principals) must complete training on (a) rater accuracy vis-à-vis the performance standards and levels (rubrics) in the teacher evaluation system and (b) procedures and processes of the teacher evaluation system

Performance management Administrators do performance ratings of teachers and provide written feedback; consulting teachers do performance ratings and mentoring of teachers
There are no examples for principals and assistant principals

Note. HR = human resources; CT = consulting teacher.

Table 3

Examples of Human Resource Alignment: Washoe County School District (Reno)

HR Practices	Examples of Alignment
1. Recruitment	
Applicant pools	New teachers are recruited from universities (e.g., University of Nevada—Reno) where students received experience with, and exposure to, the Framework for Teaching and the teacher evaluation system via classwork and internships
Information	No example available
2. Selection	
Certification	Licensure is mandatory (a 3-year provisional licensure is possible) and may require competency tests (Praxis I—academic skills assessments and preprofessional skills tests; Praxis II—principles of learning and teaching, subject assessment/specialty area tests)
Assessment	The reference check form asks the reference provider to rate the applicant on each of the four domains in the teacher evaluation system
Standards	No example available
3. Induction	
Preservice	Mandatory program—Jump Start for Success—that provides exposure to the four domains, especially classroom management
On-the-job	Principal has discussion with the teacher about the teacher evaluation system in first preobservation session
4. Mentoring	Mentors work one-on-one with novice teachers. New mentors receive training that is focused on the four domains in the teacher evaluation system. Training emphasizes observation, conversation, and feedback regarding teacher performance
5. Professional development	
Content	All professional development and inservice courses must relate to the four domains of the teacher evaluation system
	There is a 3-year sequence of coursework for new teachers built on the four domains of the teacher evaluation system
	The district partners with a state-funded regional professional development program that provides standards-based course work in curriculum content, lesson design, and assessment of student classroom learning

120

Teacher planning	Each year, teachers complete a personal inventory tool to help gauge their mastery of teaching standards and standards-based instructional design, classroom assessment, and use of standards to improve student learning Teacher learning teams in each school analyze teachers' learning needs and help plan out teacher learning via the four domains in the teacher evaluation system
6. Compensation	
Base pay	No examples available
Variable pay	Salary progression is linked to professional development and inservice coursework, which in turn are linked to the four domains of the teacher evaluation system Teachers receive an 8% base pay increase for certification by the National Board for Professional Teaching Standards during the certification period
Hiring packages	No examples available
7. Performance management	
Teacher evaluation	Teacher evaluation system is derived from the Framework for Teaching. The teachers are evaluated in four domains (Planning and Preparation, The Classroom Environment, Instruction, and Professional Responsibilities), which contain 23 performance standards. For each standard there is a 4-point rating scale depicting four levels of performance using behavioral descriptors (rubrics) to help the evaluator make a rating judgment. Judgments are made on the basis of multiple sources of evidence. Evaluators have received training in the teacher evaluation system
Feedback/Coaching	The evaluator must provide the teacher written feedback about the ratings, using standards language couched in the teacher evaluation system More informal feedback and coaching is provided by teacher learning teams, mentors, and site trainers
Goal setting	At the beginning of the year, teachers set performance goals in each of the domains of the teacher evaluation system with their evaluator
Remediation	A poor-performing teacher is placed on a focused assistance plan for improving performance in the four domains of the teacher evaluation system
8. Instructional leaders	
Selection	No examples available
Training	The district's leadership academy provides an overview of the teacher evaluation system, plus more in-depth courses about evaluation New principals and assistant principals hired from outside the district receive training in the teacher evaluation system as part of a required course they must take at the University of Nevada—Reno
Performance management	The human resources staff monitors leaders use of the teacher evaluation system and completion of all evaluations

121

Discussion

We created an HR alignment model to visually portray the links between student achievement, teacher performance competency, and instructional, and especially HR, practices. We then used the model to guide the conduct of qualitative studies of the HR practices in the Cincinnati and Washoe County school districts with a focus on capturing all the examples of HR practices for which some vertical and horizontal alignment had occurred.

In both Cincinnati and Washoe County, the Framework for Teaching was first adopted as the teacher competency model that was the foundation for a new, standards-based teacher evaluation system. Over time, other HR practices were adapted or created to become aligned with the teacher performance competency model (vertical alignment) and with each other (horizontal alignment). In neither district was there a strategic plan and coordinated unfolding of a set of initiatives to create alignment; rather, alignment occurred in mostly isolated spurts within the eight HR practices areas.

Vertical alignment represents HR practices that focus on, measure, enable, and reinforce predicted or actual teacher behavior on the performance competencies in the Framework for Teaching. We found vertical alignment in both districts to be highly developed (although evolving) in the HR practice area of performance management, particularly the teacher evaluation system and the observation and measurement parts of it. There was less alignment in the coaching/feedback and goal-setting components of performance management. Interestingly, in both sites, vertical alignment for all components of instructional leadership was in its infancy. These components will need to be developed quickly because it is difficult to sustain a performance management system and culture that includes teachers but not their instructional leaders. There was divergence in HR practice alignment as well as between the two districts. In Cincinnati, there was relatively greater emphasis on alignment of recruitment and selection, whereas in Washoe County, mentoring and especially professional development were more aligned. Finally, in both districts, there were some HR practice components for which no examples of alignment could be found.

Horizontal alignment represents the degree of coupling of HR practices together in mutually supportive and reinforcing ways, thus creating potential synergistic effects of the HR practices on teacher performance competency and student achievement. In both districts, the primary horizontal alignment emanated from the teacher evaluation system, with various HR practices springing up as they became affected by that system. Orientation, mentoring, and professional development achieved the greatest horizontal alignment in both districts, representing strong interplay between instructional and HR practices generally. Compensation and instructional leadership generally achieved relatively little horizontal alignment, with a notable exception being a requirement in Washoe that only professional development activities linked to the teacher competency model would count toward educational credits and movement on the salary schedule. In Cincinnati, the proposed Teacher Quality Program would have exemplified substantial alignment had it been implemented.

Although the HR alignment analysis is in its infancy, we think that it has interesting implications for both practice and research. For practice, the HR alignment model can serve as a strategic template to be used to guide the design and implementation of an aligned HR system. Once the district agrees on a model of performance competencies that set out what teachers need to know and to be able to do to meet student achievement goals, appropriate staff can design or redesign each HR subprogram to acquire, develop, recognize, and reward or retain the competencies. Alternately, the HR alignment model could be used to guide the evaluation of a district's current HR system, seeking to identify alignment strengths and weaknesses and then developing a strategic plan for enhancing alignment. Alignment analysis might begin by having a committee of teachers, administrators, and program specialists review each HR subsystem and make judgments about the specific performance competencies each is designed to foster. The competency lists for each subsystem could then be compared to determine how well the subsystems are aligned around a common competency model. An assessment of the degree to which the subsystems are aligned as implemented can then be done by surveying the users (see Heneman, Huett, Lavigna, & Ogsten, 1995, for an example). If alignment is low, the district may want to redesign some of the HR subsystems taking into account cost, time, and urgency concerns.

For research, HR alignment analysis might seek to develop more quantitative measures of HR practices and their degree of vertical and horizontal alignment. A checklist of examples of aligned HR practices might be developed, for example, to indicate the presence on absence of each practice (e.g., does the district use or not use a structured behavioral interview with questions derived from a teacher performance competency model?). Such measures could then be used in large, across district studies of the empirical relations between the degree of HR alignment and student achievement.

Finally, given the exploratory nature of this study, we suggest several caveats. First, we studied HR alignment to a particular teacher performance competency model for which there is favorable content and criterion-related validity. Other performance competency models might be used for HR alignment analysis; we hope that those models are backed by supportive validity evidence. We see little usefulness in studying HR alignment with nonvalid or nonvalidated teacher performance competency models. Second, we studied a competency model whose validity related to student achievement, ignoring other important student outcomes (e.g., attendance, retention). There may very well be a need for different teacher competencies and aligned HR practices to achieve these other outcomes. Third, we focused only on HR alignment intent, ignoring implementation and impact. Problems in implementation will likely limit the degree of operational HR alignment present in the two districts. Fourth, we have focused on HR alignment for performance competency only, ignoring the increasingly important outcome of teacher retention (National Commission on Teaching and America's Future, 2003). Because teacher performance competency and turnover may not be closely linked, a separate HR alignment analysis may be necessary for retention. Last, we have not addressed the structural issue of whether all eight HR practice areas should be located administratively within a single HR management unit. In both districts, for example, professional development was split off from the HR function. We have not assessed the implications of this for vertical and horizontal alignment. It seems likely that such structural segmentation will create isolated, fragmented HR practices that lack cohesion and common focus. Such threats to horizontal alignment will lessen the synergy and impact of HR practices on teacher performance competency.

References

Batt, R. (2002). Managing customer services: Human resource practices, quit rates, and sales growth. *Academy of Management Journal, 45,* 587–598.

Becker, B., & Huselid, M. A. (1998). High performance work systems and firm performance: A synthesis of research and managerial implications. *Research in Personnel and Human Resource Management, 16,* 53–101.

Danielson, C. (1996). *Enhancing professional practice: A framework for teaching.* Alexandria, VA: Association for Supervision and Curriculum Development.

Darling-Hammond, L., & Youngs, P. (2002). Defining "highly qualified teachers": What does "scientifically-based research" actually tell us? *Educational Researcher, 31*(9), 13–25.

Gallagher, H. A. (2004/this issue) Vaughn Elementary's innovative teacher evaluation system: Are teacher evaluation scores related to growth in student achievement? *Peabody Journal of Education, 79*(4), 79–107.

Gratton, L., & Truss, C. (2003). The three-dimensional people strategy: Putting human resources policies into action. *Academy of Management Executive, 17*(3), 74–96.

Heneman, H. G., III, & Judge, T. A. (2003). *Staffing organizations 4/e.* Middleton, WI: McGraw-Hill/Mendota House.

Heneman, H. G., III, Huett, D. L., Lavigna, R., & Ogsten, D. (1995). Assessing managers' satisfaction with staffing services. *Personnel Psychology, 48,* 163–172.

Kimball, S. M., White, B., Milanowski, A. T., & Borman, G. (2004/this issue). Examining the relationship between teacher evaluation and student assessment results in Washoe County. *Peabody Journal of Education, 79*(4), 54–78.

Mendro, R. L. (1998). Student achievement and school and teacher accountability. *Journal of Personnel Evaluation in Education, 12,* 257–267.

Milanowski, A. T. (2004/this issue). The relation between teacher performance evaluation scores and student achievement: Evidence from Cincinnati. *Peabody Journal of Education, 79*(4), 33–53.

National Commission on Teaching and America's Future. (2003). *No dream denied: A pledge to America's children.* Washington, DC: Author.

No Child Left Behind Act of 2001, Pub. L. No. 107–110, 115 Stat. 1425. (2002).

Rowan, B., Correnti, R., & Miller, R. J. (2002). What large-scale, survey research tells us about teacher effects on student achievement: Insights from the *Prospects* study of elementary schools. *Teachers College Record, 104,* 1525–1567.

Schippman, J. S. (1999). *Strategic job modeling.* Mahwah, NJ: Lawrence Erlbaum Associates, Inc.

Wright, P. M., Dunford, B. B., & Snell, S. A. (2001). Human resources and the resource-based view of the firm. *Journal of Management, 27,* 701–721.

Wright, S. P., Horn, S. P., & Sanders, W. L. (1997). Teacher and classroom context effects on student achievement: Implications for teacher evaluation. *Journal of Personnel Evaluation in Education, 11,* 57–67.

PEABODY JOURNAL OF EDUCATION, 79(4), 126–137
Copyright © 2004, Lawrence Erlbaum Associates, Inc.

Lessons Learned About Standards-Based Teacher Evaluation Systems

Allan Odden

Consortium for Policy Research in Education
University of Wisconsin–Madison

In this article, I draw several lessons learned about how to assess student, classroom, and teacher effects, with a specific focus on performance-based teacher evaluations. One lesson is that hierarchical linear modeling techniques are helpful in sorting out the magnitude of impacts at these three different levels of the education system. The other major lessons are reflected in the conclusion that research findings suggest that educators have learned how to design and operate performance-based teacher assessments that have sufficient reliability and validity to use for consequential decisions such as triggering pay increases.

Our CPRE research team had several interconnected objectives in conducting the research presented in the preceding five articles in this issue.

The research reported in this article was supported by a grant from the U.S. Department of Education, Office of Educational Research and Improvement and the National Institute on Educational Governance, Finance, Policymaking, and Management to the Consortium for Policy Research in Education (CPRE) and the Wisconsin Center for Education Research, School of Education, University of Wisconsin–Madison (Grant OERI–R308A60003). The opinions expressed are those of the author and do not necessarily reflect the view of the National Institute on Educational Governance, Finance, Policymaking, and Management, Office of Educational Research and Improvement, U.S. Department of Education; the institutional partners of CPRE; or the Wisconsin Center for Education Research.

Requests for reprints should be sent to Allan Odden, University of Wisconsin–Madison, Consortium for Policy Research in Education, 1025 West Johnson Street, Madison, WI 53706. E-mail: arodden@wisc.edu

The Odden, Borman, and Fermanich article on student, classroom, and school effects on student learning gains presented a more comprehensive framework within which to examine the impact of any variable at these three levels on student learning gains, such as a teacher evaluation score, apart from their use, such as for salary increases, in the human resources (HR) systems of the districts or schools. The next three articles on standards-based teacher evaluation systems (Milanowski; Kimball, White, Milanowski, & Borman; Gallagher) were derived from our research on new approaches to teacher compensation and evaluation. This research has focused on whether it was possible for districts to design and operate such evaluation systems, and these articles have addressed whether the evaluation systems produced measures of teacher performance that were "valid," that is, linked to student learning gains. These articles have assessed the evaluation scores both within the frame of the Odden et al. article and within the frame of whether the findings would support using the evaluation scores for consequences, such as triggering a salary increase. Because operating such ambitious new evaluation and/or compensation systems represents significant change in the HR systems of schools and school districts, the Heneman and Milanowski article addressed issues about the comprehensiveness and strength of the HR system that surrounds these compensation and evaluation innovations. In this article, I summarize key findings from the five articles and discuss lessons learned from the research, focusing more on the implications of the research findings for using these evaluation systems in new pay systems.

Standards-based evaluation and related knowledge and skills-based pay systems are seen as strategic elements of an HR system designed to increase teacher quality in ways that boost student achievement (Odden & Kelley, 2002). A standards-based teacher evaluation system requires the following:

1. A set of teaching standards that describes in considerable detail what teachers need to know and be able to do.
2. A set of procedures for collecting multiple forms of data on teacher's performance for each of the standards.
3. A related set of scoring rubrics that provide guidance to assessors or evaluators on how to score the various pieces of data to various performance levels and a scheme to aggregate all microscores to an overall score for a teacher's instructional performance.
4. A way to use the performance evaluation results in a new knowledge- and skills-based salary schedule if the evaluation system is to be used to trigger fiscal incentives.

As Heneman and Milanowski (2004/this issue) note, moreover, a comprehensive, strategic HR management system would also use the teaching standards to guide recruitment, selection, and promotion of teachers as well as the core of a district or state's professional development system.

The theory of action behind these initiatives posits that if the teaching standards describe effective instructional strategies, then when they are implemented in the classroom, student achievement should increase. If a standards-based teacher evaluation and compensation system were operating effectively, then, one should be able to find over time that professional development opportunities would be available for teachers to learn the new instructional practices embedded in the standards; that teachers' instructional practices were conforming more to the teaching standards; and that as instruction evolved toward what was described in the standards, student performance would increase on a continuous basis. For student performance to increase, however, the teaching standards and the performance evaluation system would need to satisfy criterion-validity standards—that higher evaluation scores were in fact linked to greater learning gains on the part of students. As the preceding articles have shown, several of these elements from the theory of action are operating in the programs studied.

Performance Evaluation Systems
Can Meet Criterion Validity Standards

The first major lesson learned is that districts and schools can design and implement ambitious, performance-based teacher evaluation systems that have a substantial degree of criterion validity (see also Holtzapple, 2001, 2002). In both Cincinnati and the Vaughn charter school, where the results are or were intended to be linked to pay increases, there were strong linkages between teacher evaluation scores and student learning gains; similar but somewhat weaker and more sporadic linkages were found for the program in Washoe County. In Cincinnati and Vaughn, the Bayes residual correlations—ranging from 0.30 to 0.40—were comparable to those found in the research on the criterion validity of performance evaluations in the private sector and much higher than commonly found in education. The results have shown on average that teachers with higher evaluation scores produced more student learning gains than predicted based on prior test scores and demographic characteristics for the students in their classrooms than did other teachers with lower evaluation scores. Given that teachers were scored at four different levels of performance, the results show that average student learning gains in each higher level of performance was greater than the previous level and that the top-rated teachers—at the accomplished or distinguished levels—produced the most learning gains.

To be sure, more such research needs to be conducted, both in these sites and in other sites. One would prefer to have such validation results for all grade levels and for all four core academic subjects, whereas in three of the four sites, just reading and mathematics achievement in selected grade levels were analyzed, and one would prefer studies that cover multiple years.

Nevertheless, the results are quite encouraging about the operation of these performance evaluation systems. For many years, district and school leaders have desired an evaluation approach that could distinguish more from less effective teachers in a fair and reliable way. The systems studied make substantial progress on this front.

Moreover, the validity of these systems occurs even though they are far from perfect performance evaluation systems (Heneman & Milanowski, 2004/this issue; Kimball, 2002; Milanowski & Heneman, 2001; Milanowski et al., 2001). Because implementing these systems is a complex undertaking, many wondered whether implementation gaffs and glitches would destroy their validity; the research results show that is not the case. Despite imperfections, the three systems generally have shown an important degree of criterion-related validity. Although both districts and the Vaughn school continue to improve the operation of their sophisticated evaluation systems, they may never operate perfect systems. Nevertheless, the research has shown that even with some shortcomings, the systems have an important degree of criterion validity.

Given these validity findings, one could also conclude that these evaluation systems are quantum improvements over typical teacher evaluation systems, often called "drive-by" evaluations. Such evaluations are usually hampered by a lack of teaching standards and scoring rubrics, limited efforts to collect data, and idiosyncratic interpretation of performance areas by those doing the evaluations (Peterson, 2000). In short, despite flaws and imperfections, the performance-based teacher evaluations in these sites are vastly superior to the usual teacher evaluations in most districts around the country. They are guided by clear and specific teaching standards, gather multiple forms of data on teachers' instructional practice, have trained evaluators score the data to performance levels according to scoring rubrics, and are valid—the higher the evaluation score, the more learning gains for students in those teachers' classrooms.

All Domains Count

Reviewers of the articles asked whether all domains contributed to the power of the teacher evaluation scores, wondering whether simplifying the systems, by removing some domains, would harm statistical impacts. Milanowski (2004/this issue) conducted an analysis of this issue in Cincinnati and found that although there were intercorrelations among the domains, dropping any domain reduced the explanatory power of the score that included all four domains. So use of all domains seems in order.

Should Validity Be Assessed Controlling for Student Characteristics in Addition to Prior Achievement?

Another issue raised by several reviewers was whether control and other variables were needed in the analysis of the link between teacher evaluation scores and student learning gains or whether criterion validity required only a simple correlation of the two variables. As is clear from the preceding articles, we chose to assess the separate and independent effects of the teacher evaluation scores, controlling for some socioeconomic status (SES) factors and other important variables as is framed in the Odden et al. (2004/this issue) article. The simple correlations between the evaluation scores and student learning gains were larger than the Bayes residual correlations, but both substantiated the validity of the evaluation systems, and we are concerned over time of identifying separate and independent effects of many variables as the Odden et al. article argued.

The Systems Are "Good Enough" to Use the Results for Stakes–Pay Increases

Particularly in Cincinnati and Vaughn, the strong criterion-validity results suggest that these performance evaluation systems are good enough to use for consequential decisions such as pay increases. Evaluation results used to trigger pay increases should be fully understood by teachers, produce reliable results across multiple assessors, and be valid—that is, have positive linkages between evaluation scores and value-added student learning. In the main, the performance evaluation programs in these two places have met these requirements (see also Heneman & Milanowski, 2003; Milanowski & Heneman, 2001; Milanowski et al., 2001)

The literature on performance evaluations in both education and the private sector has shown that many systems are not understood by the individuals being evaluated, do not have reliable scores across multiple evaluators, and most important, do not meet criterion-validity standards—but often are still used for consequential decisions. Both previous research on the operation of the systems studied here (Heneman & Milanowski, 2003; Kimball, 2002; Milanowski et al., 2001) and the current validity research has shown that these systems do not have these flaws, and although in a perfect world, one would like even higher validity coefficients, our conclusion is that the validity results show that there is a clear and statistically significant link between higher evaluation scores and value-added student learning gains, thus making it reasonable to use these systems for pay increases. Further, the statistical techniques used to assess the criterion validity of these programs were state of the art (as suggested by the lead article by Odden et al., 2004/this issue) and used several SES control variables as well as other education variables that also might produce learning gains, and the evaluation scores still proved to have independent and significant impacts on student learning gains. As a result, we believe it is appropriate to use the results in a variety of ways to increase teachers' salaries.

Using the Evaluation Results for Stakes Injects Rigor Into the Evaluation Process

These and related studies of these performance evaluation systems have also shown that when the results are intended to be used for consequential decisions, districts, schools, and the evaluators are "more serious" about good implementation. Interviews with various assessors in both Cincinnati and Vaughn showed that knowing a second person would be scoring the same teacher influenced the assessor to be more careful and more consistent in producing their scores for each teacher, whereas with no second opinion, as it were, principals did not make those statements in Washoe. Both more careful attention to their scoring of each individual teacher and having two individuals involved in determining a score for each teacher led to more consistent teacher evaluation scores in Cincinnati and Vaughn. Further, each of these jurisdictions invested considerable money in training assessors in how to do their job accurately, with Cincinnati even requiring assessors to score a common, videotaped instructional episode at a specific percentage of agreement with that of an expert scorer. Washoe invested much less in training evaluators in how to score a teacher's performance, and the validity of the evaluation scores was mixed.

Multiple Assessors Enhance Reliability and Validity

Both Cincinnati and Vaughn used at least two individuals to determine a teacher's performance level, whereas only the principal or assistant principal was involved in Washoe. In Cincinnati and Vaughn, there was substantial internal consistency in each individual teacher's overall evalua-

131

tion scores, the scores were quite reliable, and the validity results were stronger. Thus, it seems that having two individuals involved in determining a performance evaluation for each individual teacher produces final scores that are "better." Because both Cincinnati intended to and Vaughn did use the results for salary decisions, the more accurate evaluation results were important, and the research has suggested that multiple assessors contributed to these more stable and accurate scores.

I should note that most organizations that engage in performance evaluation of teachers—the National Board for Professional Teachings Standards; states using the Praxis III assessment for the permanent or professional license; and Connecticut, which has developed its own performance evaluation program for teachers—have used at least two individuals to score the teacher performance data collected in the system to performance standards. Thus, the practice seems to be that when the results are to be used for real consequences, then two individuals are involved in the scoring process.

However, developers of the Connecticut system have also stated in recent presentations that after the system is up and running for several years and seasoned assessors are produced—individuals who have been scoring data to performance standards for several years—it might be possible to move to a single-person scoring system with random audits of scores to ensure consistency.[1] However, I would hasten to say that this really was not the case for Washoe, where only the principal scored teachers' performance.

A Narrowed Measure of Teaching

The Danielson (1996) Framework for Teaching, at least the versions of the Framework used in the jurisdictions studied, identifies a large range of teaching competencies but not all key aspects of effective instruction. There are important aspects of instruction that the systems studied did not measure very well or at all, including, for example

- The assessments teachers used to measure student learning.
- The feedback teachers gave to students on these assessments.
- How teachers scored student work to district or state student performance standards.

[1]R. Pecheone (the developer of the Connecticut system), personal communication, April 2003.

- Teacher reflection on the effectiveness of their instructional practice and how that reflection would lead to changes in instructional practice.
- Data on actual student achievement.

These omissions occurred largely because of the design of the data collection system, which broadly focused on classroom observations for data on instructional practices and a teacher portfolio but generally of nonclassroom activities rather than data on the just-mentioned bulleted topics. The Connecticut assessments as well as the National Board for Professional Teaching Standards' system both rely heavily on the development of an instructional portfolio organized around the teaching of a 6- to 10-day curriculum unit, including edited videos of key instructional episodes. Further, the portfolio directions for both specifically ask for the preceding kinds of key data, which generally were missing in the systems studied. We believe the power and the impact of these systems could be enhanced with the use of such portfolios, which are more effective in getting data on and thus measuring these other important aspects of a teacher's instructional practice.

Improve HR Management Systems

Finally, the article by Heneman and Milanowski (2004/this issue) on the HR systems in which two of these programs were managed concluded that these jurisdictions have made progress in HR alignment but could go much further in designing HR structures built around the core conception of teaching contained in the evaluation standards. Indeed, each of the sites included in this set of articles could create more aligned, comprehensive, and reinforcing HR systems in which all elements give complementary signals about what type of teaching matters. As those authors noted, the professional development systems for both principals and teachers had not been aligned sufficiently well, recruitment was not always focused on getting teachers with the expertise embodied in the standards, the induction systems often were weak or did not attempt to provide those new to the system with the training in the teaching desired by the district, and principal evaluations had not been changed to make full and sound implementation of the teacher evaluation system a key element a successful principal evaluation. We can only reinforce the recommendations those authors made for districts and schools to first understand that all key elements of their HR management systems should be restructured to reinforce the type of instructional practice embodied in their teaching standards and then to make the changes so that in the shortest possible time, the HR elements worked together to give the same signals about the technical core of the district and school—the instructional practices embedded in the teaching standards.

Conducting Validity Tests With a "Natural Harvest" of Data Is Hard

Initially, the Consortium for Policy Research in Education thought it would be a real advantage in terms of data collection to conduct this type of valued-added research in districts and schools that were implementing these programs, wanted to know whether the programs were valid, and basically had the teacher evaluation and student testing data needed to conduct the research. Our thought was that this natural harvest of district and school data would reduce the time it took to gather the data and position us as researchers to spend more time conducting sophisticated analysis of possible connections.

The data collection proved to be much more complicated. First, only one of the three places actually had developed a database linking students to classrooms and teachers, a key to conducting the validity analysis. In the other two jurisdictions, therefore, we had to create these linkages ourselves or work with district personnel to do so. Needless to say, this process took considerable time. Second, because all jurisdictions administered some tests every year, we had hoped to have a large sample of students with both pretests and posttests or tests for at least 2 consecutive years. In all places except the Vaughn Charter School, this also proved not to be the case, and we lost substantial student data for this reason alone; a related study (Fermanich, 2003) in another large, urban district confronted the same reality. Third, even when we could match students with teachers, in some cases it was difficult to determine if that teacher taught the student the tested subject. Fourth, oftentimes the jurisdiction had different types of tests for the 2 different years; although Test A in Year 1 could certainly serve as a pretest for a score on Test B in the 2nd year, it certainly would have been better—and probably led to more robust findings—if the two tests had been designed to measure similar content and also had been scaled to represent a progression of content knowledge.

In short, naturally harvesting the data from ongoing district data collection practices proved more difficult than predicted and actually reduced the power of any of the analyses. In one jurisdiction, we were unable to conduct a full hierarchical linear modeling (HLM) analysis because of missing data, and in the others, we conducted the analyses on a sample that was between one fourth and one third the size of the total possible sample. Obviously, this would lead us to recommend that district data collections—particularly with the new testing requirements for the federal No Child Left Behind program—be reorganized to produce a database that could facilitate analysis of learning gains classroom by classroom and teacher by teacher.

Unaligned Tests Limit Our Ability to Judge Whether Highly Rated Teachers Are Good Enough

Another major problem just alluded to was that, except for the Vaughn Charter school, the tests used were not aligned, which meant that one could not infer anything about the magnitude of the difference between a score in the 2 years of the test. For example, with tests that are aligned across grade levels, a score of 75% in Year 2 versus a score of 65% in the 1st year means that a student has learned 10 percentage points more than an average year's expected growth. This kind of information is critical to determining whether students are making "adequate yearly academic progress." However, with unaligned scores, one does not know the substantive meaning of any difference in scores between the 2 years. Although the analysis can use the 1st year's score to predict the 2nd year's score, calculate residuals from those predictions, and link the residuals to evaluation scores, an analysis conducted in all three articles, one still does not know if the residuals were large enough even for the higher performing teachers to meet ambitious goals for improving student achievement in a standards-based state or district. So we cannot tell if the standards of practice represented by the highest scores on the evaluation systems were sufficient to close the gap between existing and desired levels of student achievement in a reasonable time.

For example, if the average score on an aligned test was 35% in the 1st year, and the proficiency level was, say, 75%, then for students to show progress toward the 75% figure, each subsequent year's score would need to improve continuously from the 35% level. One could even calculate the required points of increase to attain a 10- to 12-year goal, for example. Then one could also make this level of improvement the level desired for the "proficient" teacher evaluation score. Unfortunately, the data systems for the places studied did not allow for this type of more fine-tuned analysis, so although we know higher evaluation scores were linked to larger gains in student learning, we still do not know if the larger increases were sufficient for the students to achieve at the proficiency level at some future time period, if the annual progress identified were maintained over time.

Use of HLM Techniques to Determine Impact

The validity articles have also shown the power of using advanced statistical methods, such as HLM, to assess the linkages between performance-based teacher evaluation scores and value-added student learning. These sophisticated statistical strategies add to the confidence of each author in the conclusions of their studies about the strong linkages found in their studies. These studies also reflect the newer approaches to teasing out the separate and independent impacts of various educational actions at the classroom and school levels in producing learning gains for students, as argued in the Odden et al. article. Although it would have been acceptable, on criterion related validity grounds, just to identify a simple correlation between learning gains and the teacher evaluation scores, identifying a separate and independent impact of this measure of classroom practices takes us one step further down the road of untangling which actions at which levels of the education system have what magnitude of impact on student, value-added learning.

Summary

In sum, there are promises and pitfalls in these studies for the development and use of performance-based teacher evaluations. The articles have shown that such systems can be designed and implemented with valid results, that is, in ways that do link higher evaluation scores to greater value-added student learning gains. The systems are good enough to use for consequential decisions, such as pay increases, and when they are used for stakes and trained, multiple assessors are used to determine the overall evaluation scores, those scores are likely to be more accurate, reliable, and valid than when less training of assessors is provided and single assessors are used.

At the same time, the systems could be improved. It would help if tests aligned across grade levels were used so more substantive meaning could be imputed to greater than expected student learning gains and if districts and schools designed databases up front that linked students with teachers and classrooms. Finally, if these systems were integrated into more fully developed HR systems in which all pieces of the system were designed around the concept of instruction embodied in the teaching standards, the impact of each element of the system—as well as the overall HR system itself—likely would be much greater.

However, the bottom line is that these education jurisdictions have created, have implemented, and are operating valid teacher evaluation systems. These jurisdictions know which teacher groups are producing more student learning gains than others, and the hope is that over time, this knowledge will continue to help guide the improvements of these educational systems so instruction continues to increase in quality and more and more students achieve to rigorous proficiency standards.

References

Danielson, C. (1996). *Enhancing professional practice: A framework for teaching*. Alexandria, VA: Association for Supervision and Curriculum Development.

Fermanich, M. (2003). *School resources and student achievement: The effect of school level resources on instructional practices and student outcomes in Minneapolis public schools*. Unpublished doctoral dissertation, Department of Educational Administration, School of Education, University of Wisconsin–Madison.

Gallagher, H. A. (2004). Vaughn Elementary's innovative teacher evaluation system: Are teacher evaluation scores related to growth in student achievement? *Peabody Journal of Education, 79*(4), 79–107.

Heneman, H. G., III, & Milanowski, A. (2003). Continuing assessment of teacher reactions to a standards-based teacher evaluation system. *Journal of Personnel Evaluation in Education, 17,* 173–195.

Heneman, H. G., III, & Milanowski, A. T. (2004/this issue). Alignment of human resource practices and teacher performance competency. *Peabody Journal of Education, 79*(4), 108–125.

Holtzapple, E. (2001). *Report on the validation of teachers evaluation system instructional domain ratings*. Cincinnati, OH: Cincinnati Public Schools.

Holtzapple, E. (2002, November). *Validating a teacher evaluation system*. Paper presented at the annual meeting of the American Evaluation Association, Washington, DC.

Kimball, S. M. (2002). Analysis of feedback, enabling conditions and fairness perceptions of teachers in three school districts with new standards-based evaluation systems. *Journal for Personnel Evaluation in Education, 16*, 241–268.

Kimball, S. M., White, B., Milanowski, A. T., & Borman, G. (2004/this issue). Examining the relationship between teacher evaluation and student assessment results in Washoe County. *Peabody Journal of Education, 79*(4), 54–78.

Milanowski, A. T. (2004/this issue). The relationship between teacher performance evaluation scores and student achievement: Evidence from Cincinnati. *Peabody Journal of Education, 79*(4), 33–53.

Milanowski, A., & Heneman, H. G., III. (2001). Assessment of teacher reactions to a standards-based teacher evaluation system: A pilot study. *Journal of Personnel Evaluation in Education, 15*, 193–212.

Milanowski, A., Kellor, E., Odden, A., Heneman, H. G., III, White, B., Allen, J., et al. (2001, July) *Final report on the evaluation of the 2000–2001 implementation of the Cincinnati federation of teachers/Cincinnati public schools teacher evaluation system* (Working Paper No. TC–01–3). Madison: University of Wisconsin, Wisconsin Center for Education Research, Consortium for Policy Research in Education.

No Child Left Behind Act of 2001, Pub. L. No. 107–110, 115 Stat. 1425. (2002).

Odden, A., Borman, G., & Fermanich, M. (2004/this issue). Assessing teacher, classroom, and school effects, including fiscal effects. *Peabody Journal of Education, 79*(4), 4–32.

Odden, A., & Kelley, C. (2002). *Paying teachers for what they know and can do: New and smarter compensation strategies to improve student achievement* (2nd ed.). Thousand Oaks, CA: Corwin Press.

Peterson, K. D. (2000). *Teacher evaluation: A comprehensive guide to new directions and practices*. Thousand Oaks, CA: Corwin Press.

PEABODY JOURNAL OF EDUCATION, 79(4), 138–150

Book Notes

Mark Bray (Ed.). *Comparative Education: Continuing Traditions, New Challenges, and New Paradigms*, Dordrecht, The Netherlands: Kluwer Academic, 2003, 264 pp., ISBN 1–4020–1143–1 (paperback, $50.00).

Reviewed by A. M. Arani
Department of Education
University of Mysore, India

This book contains papers linked to the work of the World Council of Comparative Education Societies (WCCES). The WCCES is an umbrella body that brings together 30 national, regional, and language-based comparative education societies and that approximately once every 3 years holds World Congresses. The chapters in this book are revised versions of works originally presented at the 11th World Congress of Comparative Education held in South Korea in 2001.

The editor, Mark Bray, is the WCCES Secretary General and is a well-known figure in the field. Bray's editorial introduction summarizes the backgrounds and perspectives of each author and chapter in the book. The underlying theoretical orientations of these chapters, although not always explicit, can be divided into three main approaches: postmodernism, transitologies, and globalization. At the same time, some of these chapters can come under the heading of culture. Bray suggests that although some of these themes have been long lasting, others have arisen relatively recently in conjunction with broader economic, political, and social evolution.

The book is divided into three main sections. In the first section, "Conceptual and Methodological Approaches," David Wilson examines the history and future prospects of comparative and international education with particular reference to the impact of globalization and information technologies. Douglas Morgan, who is an Australian Aborigine, focuses on the hegemony of Western conceptions of science in indigenous societies. Third, in a chapter that breaks methodological ground by focusing on an intersection of cross-national and internal comparisons within a small territory, Mark Bray and Yoko Yamato focus on systems of education in international schools in Hong Kong.

The second section of the book, "Political Forces and Comparative Education," contains five chapters. Wolfgang Mitter examines the effect of the collapse of Communism on educational policies in Russia, Hungary, Poland, and the Czech Republic. Tadashi Endo compares changes in two districts in Siberia and the Russian Far East. Joseph Zajda focuses on the impact of social and economic transformation on adult education in Russia since 1991. Hiroko Fujikane analyzes approaches to global education in the United States, the United Kingdom, and Japan. In the last chapter of this section, Nirmala Rao, Kai-ming Cheng, and Kirti Narain focus on how state educational policy influences primary schooling in China and India.

The third section of the book, "Cultures in Comparative Perspective," has four chapters. Meesook Kim quantifies the cultural and school grade differences in language abilities reflected in middle-class Korean and White American children's narrative skills. Diane Hoffman describes in comparative perspective contemporary American mainstream beliefs concerning children's early emotional and behavioral development. Barbara Schulte undertakes a deep etymological and semantic analysis of certain words in the Chinese language. Hiroyuki Numata focuses on a broad historical view of concepts of childhood in Western Europe and Eastern Asia.

As Wilson observes in his chapter, the impact of information and communication technologies (ICT) on comparative education has not been explored in depth. In the past, comparative education was largely limited to elites who were rich and able to travel widely. Although ICT has broadened access, it still gives more access to the rich than to the poor. Thus, it remains that even in the information age, capital is a more important asset than knowledge.

Issues of inequity are also evident in other chapters. Although Morgan mainly focuses on differences between the underlying principles of Western science and the knowledge of indigenous peoples in Australia and the South Pacific, this problem is not confined to those groups. The issue is problematic in much of Asia and other parts of the world. In her chapter, Fujikane brings out one related dimension. As she points out,

> ideas about education for international understanding became very clear through the views of UNESCO [United Nations Educational, Social, and Cultural Organization] in the aftermath of the Second World War. Creating transnational sovereignty and learning more about others, it was argued, would eventually lead to world peace ... but this idea never became a major theme in shaping school curricula, and the initial emphasis gradually lost popularity at both national and international levels. (pp. 134–135)

The question then is why organizations like UNESCO did not succeed in making a better world through education. Fujikane's answer relates to the Cold War; economic gap; injustice; and differences in social, cultural, and religious practices.

Yet these are complex issues. Educationists in UNESCO are very familiar with the situations in countries around the world. Surprisingly, in fundamentals, there is not much difference in curricula and approaches to education in Pakistan, India, Iran, Yemen, Egypt, Algeria, Palestine, Israel, the United Kingdom, Russia, and Japan. Definitely, one is not able to find even one sentence against White people (or any other race) in schoolbooks. One is not able to find a single sentence that teaches school pupils how they can prepare a bomb to use in a suicide attack or how they can use modern weapons to kill people who have only stones in their hands. In fact, formal education has no power to create huge social changes. A look at events in developing countries shows that most social, cultural, and religious leaders were not trained in formal education systems. Leaders of Islamic movements in Indonesia, Pakistan, Iran, Iraq, Lebanon, Egypt, Algeria, Afghanistan, and Palestine were trained in Islamic schools in which curricula, books, and context are totally different from those in mainstream formal education. Therefore, it is not a war between the rich and the poor or between the north and the south. This is perhaps a war between "formal education" and "informal education" or indeed is a war between Western perceptions (or in the words of Morgan, "Western knowledge") and non-Western perceptions. In Pakistan, Iraq, Saudi Arabia, Egypt, Israel, and India, religious schools train people to believe that only their religion is correct. Recently, some clergy in India took a decision advocating banning of the slaughter of cows, which provides cheap protein to millions of people. I have seen on television one great Swami saying, "Here is India and cow is holy; therefore everybody who does not like this ban may leave this country." According to his order, at least 300 million people should leave India.

Thus, the responsibility of the educationists, and especially of the comparativists, is great. Organizations like UNESCO have failed to recognize the role and power of religious schools in the previously mentioned countries, and it may be suggested that this dimension is underrecognized in the book under review. "Informal educational system," as I explained previously, can be a new area for researchers in the field of comparative education.

Nevertheless, the book contains many stimulating chapters; those in the second section of the book should be appreciated particularly. The authors make the point that political and socioeconomic forces play a vital role in shaping the education in Russia, Eastern Europe, India, and China. One of the main strengths of this section of the book is that data are collected through multiple methods of observations, interviews, and surveys, which adequately validate the presented data and can be a good example for other researchers in the field.

Peter Schrag. *Final Test: The Battle for Adequacy in America's Schools*, New York: The New Press, 2003, 250 pp., ISBN 1–5658–4821–7 (hardcover, $25.95).

Reviewed by Michael A. Rebell
Executive Director and Counsel
Campaign for Fiscal Equity, Inc.

Describing the new wave of state court adequacy litigations as "the most promising as well as the last attempt" (p. 13) to fulfill the equal educational opportunity vision of *Brown v. Board of Education,* noted journalist and author Peter Schrag has written an important new book titled *Final Test*, which comprehensively describes the origins, current status, and future directions of what the book's subtitle calls "the battle for education adequacy in America's schools."

Final Test describes in poignant detail the impact of funding inequities on individual students and why "money matters" in rectifying educational inadequacies. The heart of the book is a set of highly readable mini–case studies of recent (and in some cases still ongoing) adequacy litigations in eight states: Kentucky, California, New Jersey, Ohio, Alabama, North Carolina, Maryland, and New York. Intermixing important analytic insights, such as the effect of the elected status of judges on the ultimate outcome of the litigations in some states, with human dramas, such as the abusive cross-examination of plaintiff school children by high-powered corporate defense attorneys hired by the state of California, Schrag's overviews convey significant social commentary through delightful character sketches and engrossing stories.

Schrag's extensive research—he interviewed dozens of the educators, lawyers, and advocates leading the fight for adequacy and their opponents and personally reviewed thousands of pages of court decisions and transcripts—results in a nuanced portrait that demonstrates the powerful impact that state court litigation has on education reform throughout the country. Over the past 3 decades, after the U.S. Supreme Court declined to tackle the blatant inequities in education funding that existed in most states, advocates have turned to the state courts. In what has proved to be the most creative flowering of state constitutional law in American history, litigation has occurred in 45 states, and plaintiffs have prevailed in most of them.

Schrag extensively documents the positive impacts of many of these judicial interventions. A landmark Kentucky case led to "an alphabet soup of interlinked school reforms in every area of K–12 schooling, from governance to child care" (p. 70). In New Jersey, litigation won publicly funded preschool and full-day kindergarten for the low-income, largely minority children in the state's 30 high-need school districts as well as a comprehensive school renovation and construction program, art and music programs, and other improvements (p. 117). Methodically evenhanded, Schrag is quick to also cite examples in which political realities limited meaningful school reform as mandated by the courts such as the political manipulations and judicial about-faces that undermined an extensive court order in Alabama.

Although he creatively catalogues the major impact that court cases have had in fueling the education adequacy movement, the one major drawback in the book is the lack of a theoretical perspective for understanding the courts' role and how the positive effects of judicial intervention can be maximized. At times, he adopts the stale clichés of the "judicial activism" debate of the 1970s, such as "generalist" judges may not "be equipped to manage" complex school systems (p. 233). The fact is that judges who are successful with remedies in these cases do not presume to manage large school systems. In contrast with the way judicial interventions were handled in some of the early federal desegregation cases, state court judges in the contemporary education adequacy realm tend to promote an effective judicial–legislative dialogue that respects constitutional separation of powers precepts by ensuring that each of the branches carries out the remedial responsibilities that it is best equipped to handle.

In this dialogue, the courts' prime role is to articulate basic constitutional parameters for reform and to set serious time lines for their accomplishment. The specific funding formulas and accountability principles to implement these parameters are the responsibility of the legislative and executive branches. New York's highest court, for example, recently issued such constitutional guidelines in *Campaign for Fiscal Equity v. State of New York*. After finding the state's education finance system unconstitutional, the Court gave the governor and the legislature about a year to

1. Ascertain the actual cost of providing a sound basic education.
2. Reform the funding system to ensure that every school has the necessary level of resources.

3. Provide a system of accountability to measure whether the reforms actually provide the opportunity for a sound basic education.[1]

The governor and the legislature could adopt any one of several available methodologies for a costing out study, and any of an even larger number of funding and accountability approaches would satisfy this mandate. In other words, the political branches are accorded broad discretion to create an effective funding and accountability system so long as they promptly meet their bottom line constitutional responsibility to fairly determine and provide the amount of resources students need to obtain an adequate education.

Publication of *Final Test* could not be more timely. As the 50th anniversary of the U.S. Supreme Court's landmark desegregation decision approaches, Schrag dramatically relates the potential of the adequacy movement to the still unrealized vision of *Brown v. Board of Education*:

> For all the questions it raises, the adequacy argument is also a sophisticated and passionate declaration of faith in the great promises of American society: equality, opportunity and human and social betterment—a sine qua non for a modern technological democracy. (p. 249)

William H. Watkins. *The White Architects of Black Education: Ideology and Power in America, 1865–1954*, New York: Teachers College Press, 2001, 207 pp., ISBN 0–8077–4043–8 (cloth, $50.00).

Reviewed by Thomas V. O'Brien
School of Teaching and Learning
The Ohio State University at Mansfield

In this book, William H. Watkins scrutinizes a small group of powerful White elites who shaped the Black impulse for schooling in the postbellum America. In doing so, he builds on the historical work of James D. Anderson, Horace Mann Bond, and Ronald E. Butchart while employing critical theory.

---

[1]The references here are to *CFE v. State of New York*, 100 N.Y. 2d 893 (2003). Schrag's account of the New York case necessarily stopped before this June 2003 decision was issued.

Like these writers, Watkins approaches his study broadly and attempts to see schooling in its sociopolitical context. Watkins downplays the great migration and famous Washington–Du Bois debate over what constituted a proper schooling for the race. He sees these as minor developments compared to the thoughts and actions of "White architects" who stepped forward to offer a solution to the "Negro problem." Watkins writes about the establishment of Black schools as a social interaction between unequal groups and studies this interplay from the vantage point of the more powerful group. Thus, he casts his analysis as an expression of colonialism.

Watkins's subjects are 11 wealthy power brokers who he sees as men who were primarily interested in building profits, reducing class conflict in the South, and uplifting Blacks to the regional political economy. Watkins sketches and then evaluates the lives and impact of these architects—Samuel Chapman Armstrong, Frank Giddings, Phelps Stokes, Thomas Jesse Jones, four men from the Rockefeller family, Robert Curtis Odgen, William Henry Baldwin, and J. L. M. Curry—and successfully demonstrates how they were well connected to big business, government, and higher education. They operated at a pivotal time and place in U.S. history and saw a connection between the Negro problem and the future America. They also appreciated the significance of Black education, Watkins writes, and saw it as an arena that could be used to help them define 20th-century American society. They used their substantial clout to influence curricula and shape school policy, and this, Watkins suggests, allowed for the successful preservation of a social structure stratified by race, class, and gender. Consequently, Watkins concludes, their actions left an indelible imprint on the Black schooling, racial relations, and American ideology—marks that endure even today.

Watkins finds that his subjects were not evil but rather "forward seeking" men who were interested in the collective and private good. They recognized the need for a solution to the race issue in the wake of the Civil War and thought the proper solution could serve dual purposes: to unite the country and to lay the foundation for the emerging industrial-corporate order. Although they are cast as architects, Watkins is able to explain how philanthropic idealism, New South ideology, Darwinism, and religion shaped these men's values. Given his framework in critical theory, it comes as no surprise that Watkins is captious of his subjects as well as the enterprise and stratified society that they helped create. These architects, Watkins contends, were more than carpenters; they represented and made legitimate not only separate and unequal schooling but also a social structure of racial privilege, racial separation, and corporate capitalism. History, Watkins concludes, needs to hold these men accountable for the schools and the society they created.

Although Watkins's treatment of the architects and the political economy is compelling, two important titles are missing from his bibliography: Eric Anderson and Alfred Moss's (1999) *Dangerous Donations: Northern Philanthropy and Southern Black Education, 1902–1930* and Judith Sealander's (1997) *Private Wealth and Public Life: Foundation Philanthropy and the Reshaping of American Social Policy From the Progressive Era to the New Deal.* This is unfortunate because both books provide a nuanced interpretation of Northern philanthropy at odds with Watkins's view. Also, although Watkins mentions that Black activism played a role in tempering the architects' design, he provides no evidence to substantiate this claim. Aside from a handful of references to Du Bois and Washington, the reader learns precious little about how various designs of Black schooling were shaped by Blacks. Watkins is correct to state that Southern Blacks were far more than passive victims of well-heeled Whites, but his failure to cite primary or secondary sources to back up this point only serves to weaken his argument. What is needed here is a historically grounded discussion of how Blacks operated to influence the White architects' blueprint. Watkins would have done well to weigh sources cited by Adam Fairclough (2001) in *Teaching Equality: Black Schools in the Age of Jim Crow* and to weigh Fairclough's thesis that Black educators in the Jim Crow South were by and large discretionary agents of Black liberation. Finally, Watkins's analysis also fails to address how segregated Black schools in the North came about and established curricula.

In spite of these flaws, Watkins tells a provocative story about the growth of Black schooling between the end of the Civil War and the start of the Civil Rights movement. Watkins insists that we take stock of the key role played by a small number of powerful, behind-the-scenes men. As such, Watkins's book, when read along with the other books mentioned previously, helps to further one's understanding to the history of the growth and social purpose of Black schooling.

References

Anderson, E., & Moss, A. F. (1999). *Dangerous donations: Northern philanthropy and Southern Black education, 1902–1930.* Columbia: University of Missouri Press.

Fairclough, A. (2001). *Teaching equality: Black schools in the age of Jim Crow.* Athens: University of Georgia Press.

Sealander, J. (1997). *Private wealth and public life: Foundation philanthropy and the reshaping of American social policy from the progressive era to the new deal.* Baltimore: Johns Hopkins University Press.

Rexford G. Brown. *It's Your Fault: An Insider's Guide to Learning and Teaching in City Schools*, New York: Teachers College Press, 2003, 168 pp., ISBN 0–8077–4379–8 (paperback, $16.95).

Reviewed by Christina Hart
Department of Leadership, Policy, and Organizations
Peabody College of Vanderbilt University

For anyone who works in the front lines of the public education system who has ever wanted to say "it's your fault" to the uninformed policymakers, the out-of-touch university faculty, the uninvolved parent, and all other finger-pointing educational naysayers, this book is for you. Rexford Brown has written an entertaining, clever, anecdotal account of a behind-the-scenes look at the realities of modern public schools.

In an intensely personal manner, Brown gets to the core of serious issues surrounding America's schools: the special education system; the effects of educational bureaucracy; and the roles of the principal as a leader, the teacher as a professional, the parent as a parent, and the student as a learner. All of these issues are unfolded in a compilation of personal essays with witty titles such as "On Leading, Misleading, and Unleading," "Full Moon Over Middle School," and "Serving Time." The essay titles capture the almost comical nature Brown uses to invite the reader to join him as he details a thoughtful and insightful exploration of what it is really like to participate in a bureaucratic school system that he likens to an early 20th-century factory concerned with outputs and consumed with the conviction that time is money.

Each essay highlights hard questions and provides some commonsense answers concerning how to tackle tough educational issues through a lens that would focus on principles of learning. One issue for which Brown offers a particularly detailed account is that of special education. Brown follows the experiences of a special education student as she and her parents navigate their way through the convolutions and rigidities of a policies formulated as a result of formal legal compliance. Brown questions the extent to which the very laws that are designed to help developmentally disabled students are actually hurting them, as educational stakeholders struggle to meet the needs of an ever-increasing number of students diagnosed with learning and emotional disorders.

Another topic that Brown examines with surprising candor and insight is the degree to which educational stakeholders are held hostage to the rigorous pace of a time-based education system. Brown speaks to the heart of an issue that every educator knows is true when he describes how schools are designed not as organizations of learning but instead as bureaucracies that are "so tightly organized around time" that the principles of effective teaching and learning are secondary. By comparing America's school systems with the structure and operations of a mechanistic/bureaucratic organization that typifies a factory, Brown convincingly argues how these schools are suffering from an organizational form centered on time rather than what is known about learning.

In the essay that is the namesake of the book, Brown "takes no prisoners" as he scolds everyone involved with schooling. Brown asks the teachers to stop whining and to act professional, the students to cease with their narcissistic attitudes, the policymakers to consider eliminating some laws, and the board members to drop their political agendas and get in touch with the realities of the school. It is in this essay that Brown's humor succeeds magnificently in connecting with experienced educators as he puts into print the very criticisms and concerns that so many teachers and administrators have about their profession.

Throughout the book, Brown shares many of the thoughts educators often have about students, parents, fellow employees, board members, policymakers, administrators, and themselves—thoughts that are not shared outside of the faculty lounge perhaps because they are too revealing or too commonsensical to warrant serious consideration. Brown's wit is engaging, and the reader is easily drawn into the inside world of educators. Although Brown addresses some politically, socially, and educationally dicey topics, he does so in a tone that is inoffensive and approachable.

Because the book is limited to Brown's personal account of the major issues surrounding today's schools, there is no hint of validation for alternative opinions or differing sides of the major issues. However, Brown should not be condemned for this. This book is, after all, a personal account, and Brown is entitled to vent his positions. It is in these positions that the insight only an experienced educator and administrator can offer becomes apparent. Brown reflects on his real-world experiences as a director of a charter school he started and as a policy analyst and produces some very poignant observations about the state of modern public education. Brown's professional and personal experiences provide him with a credibility that firms the ground on which he stakes his opinions and suggestions. What is appealing about Brown's style is a bold sense of how to think about and convey the realities of working in a modern school in a humorous yet serious manner.

The intent of this book is not to develop a theory or contribute to educational research. Rather, it can best be described as an entertaining, fresh look at the realities of modern public schools. The one fault of the book is Brown's attempt to limit the applicability of his insights to urban schools. One could make a strong argument that these challenges are of consequence to some degree in all public schools.

Mark Bray (Ed.). *Comparative Education: Continuing Traditions, New Challenges, and New Paradigms,* Dordrecht, The Netherlands: Kluwer Academic, 2003, 264 pp., ISBN 1–4020–1143–1 (paperback, $50.00).

Reviewed by Stephen P. Heyneman
Department of Leadership, Policy, and Organizations
Peabody College of Vanderbilt University

Since its founding, comparative education has struggled with a problem of identity. Is it a compendium of interests in education, internationally applied? Or is it a discipline in itself with unique traditions of scholarship? If the former, it would include all educational applications of the social sciences (anthropology, economics, political science, sociology, history, psychology, etc.), all educational applications of the professional disciplines (law, school administration, university administration, public policy and management, curriculum and instruction, teaching and learning, and technology), and all the concerns of specific nations and/or regions (Africa, Latin America, postconflict environments, postparty states, and the like). If comparative education consists of all this, what might it leave out? On the other hand, if comparative education is a discipline with a specialized set of interests deserving of an independent and autonomous position among other disciplines, then what are those disciplines and what is their future?

This new book on comparative education consists of a dozen essays chosen by editor Mark Bray from among 390 papers presented at an international meeting of the World Council of Comparative Education. The essays previously appeared in a special issue of *International Review of Education.* Given the plethora of topics that could fit under the comparative education umbrella and the difficulty of finding papers of minimal standards from an international conference, one might be excused for having fairly low expectations of the product. However, this one is worth reading.

Following an introductory essay, the chapters are divided into three sections covering methods, political forces, and cultures. The result does not answer the basic comparative education dilemma. Faculty will not be able to use this book as a basic text. What makes this book compelling, however, is that most of the essays are interesting.

For instance, under the methodology section, there is a discussion that compares achievement, cost, and quality of the 47 international schools in Hong Kong. Are German schools better than French schools? One need not go to France or Germany when their schools may be in America's backyard. There is a chapter that provides a synthesis of international comparisons over the last 200 years, the author arguing that because comparison was so deeply influential in the era of the fountain pen, will it not be more influential with the methods from the Internet and the computerized library information systems?

With respect to political forces, three of the five chapters in this section concentrate on changes following the end of the party/state in Eastern Europe and the former Soviet Union. Deeply knowledgeable about the region, one author reflects on the profoundly important common processes—decentralization of management; privatization of financing; structural and curricular reforms; and the rapid introduction of standardized evaluation, testing, and selection. A more in-depth application are those in a second chapter that describes how these changes have affected Siberia and the Russian Far East. A third chapter on lifelong learning in Russia is also a surprise. The author correctly observes that the adult education "push" from within the Soviet system was surprisingly backward (in pedagogy, efficiency, and purpose) when compared to the norms of the West. What happened after this system had to confront the emptiness of its prior claims? Perhaps the most interesting chapter in this group is the one that compares the educational performance of China and India since the 1940s. China has outperformed India on almost every indicator, but is this because the role of the state under central planning was so different or because the underlying cultural attitude toward education was so different?

With respect to culture, there is an essay on differences between Korean and White American children in how they develop effective narrative skills when one culture emphasizes speaker competence and the other emphasizes listener competence. There is a chapter on what children have lost by educational modernization in both Europe and Japan. The author argues that in the Middle Ages, children had a miserable life, but in the 18th century, childhood was discovered by social scientists and social workers who established childhood as a period for protection. The author argues that childhood has returned to its previous level of low expectations and high pressure in both Europe and Japan, illustrated by the examination hell in which young students study for unconscionable periods of time and universally suffer adverse consequences.

It would not be true to suggest that these chapters are of uniform quality. In one, the author argues that traditional peoples of Africa, Latin America, and Asia should have university programs dedicated to their own particular wisdom because it is totally different from Western disciplinary traditions (so much for anthropology). In another, the social hierarchy and the word for *work* in Chinese is said to have profound implications for vocational education. Neither chapter seems to be worth much attention.

Some of the virtue in this book lies in the diverse background of the scholar authors. For many years, the editor has been responsible for insights on education in China, Europe, and the United States from afar. The analysis of the Soviet Far East is through a Japanese perspective. The tendency in the post–Soviet world is from a German. The comparison of China and India is by a partnership from each country. If the future of comparative education were to depend less on its definition and more on the quality of interest and insight, then these essays would bode very well for the discipline.

www.ingramcontent.com/pod-product-compliance
Ingram Content Group UK Ltd.
Pitfield, Milton Keynes, MK11 3LW, UK
UKHW020429010325